INSIGHT ⊙ GUIDES

EXPLORE

JERUSALEM
& TEL AVIV

PLAN & BOOK
YOUR TAILOR-MADE TRIP

BRAZIL   **CHILE**   **ECUADOR**

TAILOR-MADE TRIPS & UNIQUE EXPERIENCES CREATED BY LOCAL TRAVEL EXPERTS AT INSIGHTGUIDES.COM/HOLIDAYS

Insight Guides has been inspiring travellers with high-quality travel content for over 45 years. As well as our popular guidebooks, we now offer the opportunity to book tailor-made private trips completely personalised to your needs and interests.
By connecting with one of our local experts, you will directly benefit from their expertise and local know-how, helping you create memories that will last a lifetime.

HOW INSIGHTGUIDES.COM/HOLIDAYS WORKS

STEP 1

Pick your dream destination and submit an inquiry, or modify an existing itinerary if you prefer.

STEP 2

Fill in a short form, sharing details of your travel plans and preferences with a local expert.

STEP 3

Your local expert will create your personalised itinerary, which you can amend until you are completely satisfied.

STEP 4

Book securely online. Pack your bags and enjoy your holiday! Your local expert will be available to answer questions during your trip.

BENEFITS OF PLANNING & BOOKING AT INSIGHTGUIDES.COM/HOLIDAYS

PLANNED BY LOCAL EXPERTS
The Insight Guides local experts are hand-picked, based on their experience in the travel industry and their impeccable standards of customer service.

SAVE TIME & MONEY
When a local expert plans your trip, you save time and money when you book, even during high season. You won't be charged for using a credit card either.

TAILOR-MADE TRIPS
Book with Insight Guides, and you will be in complete control of the planning process, from the initial selections to amending your final itinerary.

BOOK & TRAVEL STRESS-FREE
Enjoy stress-free travel when you use the Insight Guides secure online booking platform. All bookings come with a money-back guarantee.

WHAT OTHER TRAVELLERS THINK ABOUT TRIPS BOOKED AT INSIGHTGUIDES.COM/HOLIDAYS

Trip to Portugal

Every step of the planning process and the trip itself was effortless and exceptional. Our special interests, preferences and requests were accommodated resulting in a trip that exceeded our expectations.

Corinne, USA   ★★★★★

Trip to Vietnam

The organization was superb, the drivers professional, and accommodation quite comfortable. I was well taken care of! My thanks to your colleagues who helped make my trip to Vietnam such a great experience.

Heather   ★★★★★

DON'T MISS OUT
BOOK NOW AT
INSIGHTGUIDES.COM/HOLIDAYS

CONTENTS

BEACHES

Tel Aviv has 14km (8 miles) of beaches; Israel has a Mediterranean coastline that stretches for 273km (170 miles). Explore Tel Aviv's beaches (route 7) and its northern coastline (route 12).

RECOMMENDED ROUTES FOR...

FOODIES

Sample Israel's unique culinary fusion in Jerusalem's Makhanei Yehuda market (route 3), or Tel Aviv's Kerem Hatamanim (route 10).

HISTORY BUFFS

Israel is as much about history as it is religion. Visit the Herodian fortress of Masada (route 6), the historic village of Ein Kerem (route 5) and the ancient ports of Caesarea and Akko (route 12).

MARKETS

Practice your bartering skills at Jerusalem's Arab market (route 1), immerse yourself in the sensory paradise of Makhanei Yehuda market (route 3) or tour Tel Aviv's markets (route 10) in search of hidden gems.

MUSEUMS

Visit the Israel Museum in Jerusalem to see the Dead Sea scrolls (route 4) and the Museum of the Jewish People in Tel Aviv (route 11) to experience the story of the Diaspora.

NIGHT OWLS

Tel Aviv is the city that never sleeps. For the best nightlife, try the western end of Rothschild Boulevard (route 9), Tel Aviv Port (route 7) or Jerusalem's Makhanei Yehuda (route 3).

SACRED SITES

Israel is the Holy Land and Jerusalem is the Holy City. The Old City (route 1) and the Galilee (route 13) take in the most sacred sites.

VIEWS

Israel is a country of hills and breathtaking panoramas. Get a unique perspective of Jerusalem from the Mount of Olives (route 2), look out over Haifa from the Bahá'í Gardens (route 12) and take in the Sea of Galilee from Mount Tabor (route 13). Don't miss the stunning Dead Sea landscapes (route 6).

INTRODUCTION

An introduction to Jerusalem and Tel Aviv's geography, customs and culture, plus illuminating background information on cuisine, history and what to do when you're there.

Tel Aviv's seafront

EXPLORE JERUSALEM & TEL AVIV

Jerusalem prays while Tel Aviv plays. A 30-minute drive separates Israel's two largest cities, yet they are worlds apart. Sacred and profane, Jerusalem and Tel Aviv represent the country's religious past and its high-tech future.

Jerusalem is as old as Tel Aviv is new. Sacred to Judaism, Christianity, and Islam, the alleyways of Jerusalem's Old City resonate with three millennia of religious significance, from the remnants of King Solomon's Temple, to Christ's last journey down the Via Dolorosa, to the Dome of the Rock, from where it is believed Mohammed ascended to heaven.

Outside the city walls, Jerusalem is home to its parliament and national institutions, and has been revived over the past century by the Jewish return to Zion. Controversy shrouds Jerusalem's status as Israel's capital; both Israelis and Palestinians regard the city as their capital. Whilst Jerusalem is not universally recognised in the world as Israel's capital, Israelis feel passionately that it should be. It is a city of nearly 1 million, fiercely contested by the Israeli majority and Palestinian minority, home to a socially fragmented Jewish population, from the fast-growing black-hat ultra-Orthodox enclaves, through an array of modern-Orthodox and traditional communities and onto a dwindling secular minority. Yet the city hangs together in an uneasy truce with a surprising degree of harmony and an even more surprising flourishing nightlife scene.

In contrast, Tel Aviv, Israel's commercial capital, the capital of cool, is brazen and brash. It is the city that never stops, from its golden beaches and glistening high-tech office towers, to its innovative culinary and cultural scene and pulsating nightlife. Tel Aviv itself has a population of 550,000, and is at the heart of a metropolitan area that is home to over 4 million.

GEOGRAPHY AND LAYOUT

The contrasting characteristics of Tel Aviv and Jerusalem are also reflected in their geography and layout. Although a relatively small country – roughly the size of New Jersey or Wales – Israel is geographically diverse. Tel Aviv is on the fertile coastal plain while beyond the orange groves and vineyards of the inland plains and foothills, Jerusalem is 750 meters (2,500ft) high in the Judean Mountains. Jerusalem is a continental divide with forests to the west leading down to the Mediterranean, and

Dome of the Rock, Jerusalem

deserts to the east leading down to the Dead Sea, the lowest accessible point on earth, and part of the Great Syria-African Rift Valley.

Labyrinth and grid

City streets in Jerusalem and Tel Aviv are also contrasting. Jerusalem's narrow, labyrinthine streets and alleys coil confusingly around hillsides, up to breathtaking mountain views of desert and forest; Tel Aviv is laid out in US-style grid fashion with wide avenues and Parisian-style boulevards running north–west parallel to the Mediterranean seafront, or east–west.

DAY TRIPS TO THE REST OF ISRAEL

The rest of Israel is easily accessible from Jerusalem and Tel Aviv. Head north from Tel Aviv along the Mediterranean coast to the port of Haifa, which is built on Mount Carmel and is the world center of the Bahá'í Faith, with its sumptuous hillside gardens. Further north is the ancient port and Crusader fortress city of Akko. Inland are the mountain landscapes of the Galilee hills, Nazareth and Sea of Galilee, fed by the River Jordan, which is where Christ spent the majority of his life. To the east, you'll find the Golan Heights and majestic snow-capped Mount Hermon.

Just south of Jerusalem, in the Palestinian territories, is Bethlehem,

birthplace of Christ; to the east is the Dead Sea, where bathers can float in the highly saline waters. Several hours south through the desert is the Red Sea resort of Eilat, a diverse paradise with its remarkable marine life and coral formations.

HISTORY

Archeological evidence suggests that farming evolved in this region some 12,000 years ago and there are remains of human settlements on the Mediterranean coast, Judean Desert, and Jordan Valley. Canaanite city kingdoms developed in the heart of the 'fertile crescent,' along trading routes between the two regional powers – Egypt and Mesopotamia. Genesis tells us that Abraham moved here

Praying at the Western Wall

Nightlife in Jerusalem

from Mesopotamia in about 2000 BC, settling in Be'er Sheva and buried in Hebron. According to the book of Exodus, after his descendants went into exile in Egypt as slaves, they returned under Moses, and then Joshua, to re-conquer the country.

Jerusalem

3,000 years ago, King David moved his capital from Hebron to a new city, which he built on a mountaintop above a spring 29km (18 miles) to the north and named Jerusalem. His son, King Solomon, built the First Temple, which was rebuilt after the Babylonian conquest and ultimately destroyed by the Romans, shortly after Christ's crucifixion. In the 4th century, Roman Emperor Constantine's mother, Helena, identified the city's Christian holy sites. There followed the Islamic, Crusader, Mameluke, and Ottoman conquests.

The Old City, within the walls built by Ottoman ruler Suleiman the Magnificent in the 16th century, is divided into Jewish, Christian, Muslim, and Armenian quarters, and contains the city's major sacred sites. It was only from the mid-19th century that the city spread outside of the walls, as European Jews began immigrating to the Holy City, and European imperial powers built a presence. The British took control of Jerusalem in 1917. After Israeli independence in 1948, the city was divided, with West Jerusalem declared Israel's capital. The city was reunited in 1967 when Israel captured East Jerusalem from Jordan during the Six-Day War.

Tel Aviv

From 1909, the sand dunes to the north of Jaffa were transformed into an affluent garden suburb, although Tel Aviv is far more than a century old. Biblical Jaffa is one of the world's oldest ports and Neve Tsedek, which links Jaffa to Tel Aviv, was established in 1887. Tel Aviv was further developed in the 1930s by German immigrants fleeing Nazi persecution, who introduced Bauhaus architecture. David Ben-Gurion declared the city's independence here in 1948, but in the ensuing years the city became rundown as waves of penniless immigrants arrived. But Israel's famous high-tech industry and start-up culture have seen the city emerge as one of the world's financial centers. It is also the city that never stops, with golden Mediterranean beaches, a world-famous culinary scene, and pulsating nightlife.

CLIMATE

For a small country, Israel has very diverse climate zones. Tel Aviv on the coastal plain and Jerusalem in the mountains have different climates. Israeli summers are long – from April to October – hot, and virtually rainless. During these months, Tel Aviv

Makhanei Yehuda market *Floating in the Dead Sea*

and the coast are humid (average 70 percent), while the atmosphere in hill towns such as Jerusalem is drier and much cooler (average 30 percent). Because Jerusalem is in the hills, summer evenings can be pleasantly cool. While Tel Aviv has a mild winter, Jerusalem can get very cold, with frosty nights but long spells of sunshine. Both cities have very heavy winter rainfall.

With average summer temperatures above 86°F (30°C), March/April and October/November are the ideal time to visit, with average temperatures of 70°F (21°C), and mainly dry, sunny weather.

POPULATION

With an annual growth rate of 2 percent Israel's population reached 9 mil-

---

DON'T LEAVE ISRAEL WITHOUT...

Seeing the Holy Sites. Within the walls of Jerusalem's Old City are sites sacred to Jews, Christians, and Muslims. Visit the Western Wall, the only remnant of the Second Temple. Walk along the Via Dolorosa to the site of Christ's crucifixion and resurrection in the Church of the Holy Sepulchre. Explore the Temple Mount where Mohammed prayed in the Al Aksa Mosque and ascended to heaven from the exquisite Dome of the Rock.

Visiting the Israel Museum. Israel's national museum includes impressive collections of archeology, art, and Judaica, with pride of place going to the Dead Sea Scrolls, the oldest known version of the Old Testament.

Walking through Makhanei Yehuda Market. By day Jerusalem's market is a delight of fresh produce and garrulous vendors. By night it transforms into a lively collections of bars and street food outlets.

Floating in the Dead Sea. The excessively salty water means that you miraculously float on the surface of the sea. If you have any energy left, climb Masada, Herod's former fortress, for a breathtaking view of the sea and desert.

Strolling along Tel Aviv seafront. From Jaffa Port in the south to Tel Aviv Port in the north, the city's golden beaches are a must for vacationers. Stop for a glass of wine and watch the sun set over the Mediterranean.

Eating a vegan meal. Tel Aviv is famous for its vegan cuisine, which creatively overcomes the need to forego fish, meat, dairy, and eggs.

Spending a night on the town in Tel Aviv. Known as the city that never stops, Tel Aviv's nightlife exudes the most marvellous energy. From Jaffa's flea market, to Florentine and all along the seafront, the city revels into the early hours.

Climbing Haifa's Bahá'í Hillside Gardens. Billed as the world's longest hillside gardens, they also offer a fantastic view of Haifa Bay.

lion in 2019. Israel has a 25 percent Arab minority, while the 75 percent Jewish majority is highly fragmented between secular, Orthodox and black-hat ultra-Orthodox Jews and waves of Jewish immigrants from Central and Eastern Europe, North Africa and the Middle East, Ethiopia and elsewhere. There are also some 300,000 migrant workers and refugees in the country, mostly from Africa, the Philippines and Latin America.

Jerusalem's population mix is distinctly different from the rest of the country: about 35 percent of its 950,000 residents are Palestinian Arabs (34 percent Muslims and 1 percent Christian), 45 percent of the population are Orthodox Jews (25 percent ultra-Orthodox and 20 percent modern Orthodox), and the remaining 20 percent are secular Jews. However, most of the more conservative Arab and ultra-orthodox populations tend to stick to their own neighborhoods, giving a more secular and modern feel to the city. The Palestinian, and especially the ultra-Orthodox, communities have a much higher birth rate, and are becoming larger forces in the city by the year.

Tel Aviv, in contrast, is a predominantly secular Jewish city. The clear majority of the city's 550,000 residents are secular. Although there are bastions of ultra-Orthodoxy in neighboring cities like Bnei Brak, most people in the metropolitan area of 4 million are also secular.

LOCAL CUSTOMS

Israel is best known for its informality and this extends to both Jerusalem and Tel Aviv. People tend to dress casually, even to business meetings. However, there is a major contrast between the two cities in terms of female modesty. In hedonistic Tel Aviv, anything goes, but in Jerusalem, especially when visiting the holy sites or the ultra-Orthodox quarter of M'ea She'arim, modest dress is mandatory.

Most Israelis speak English and take pleasure in practicing their language skills with foreign visitors. In the age of air-conditioning, the siesta is no longer an inextricable part of the Mediterranean culture. Even so, nightlife begins late, with bars and clubs not getting busy until after 10pm and both Jerusalem (try the Makhane Yehuda market) and Tel Aviv buzzing until way past 2am.

POLITICS AND ECONOMICS

Israel is a democracy with a 120-member Knesset (parliament) elected every four years by all citizens over 18 on a proportional representation basis. Israel's leftist Labor Party controlled government until 1977, while the right-wing Likud has ruled for most of the time since. The president, elected by Knesset members, is a titular head of state, not dissimilar to the British monarch. The Supreme Court has the power to interpret Knesset legislation.

Jerusalem's Old City

Israel has a Western European standard of living, with a per capita GDP slightly below that of the UK and France. The driving force behind the economy is high-tech in areas such as biotech, clean technology, IT, communications, defense electronics, Internet of things, and artificial intelligence.

Despite the country's fragmented social composition and religious-ethnic divisions, Israelis are a surprisingly harmonious and hospitable people, with enormous goodwill to tourists, with whom they are eager to converse and host.

TOP TIPS FOR EXPLORING JERUSALEM AND TEL AVIV

Respect the sun. It may only be 77°F (25°C) in the shade but Israel is far south so sunstroke, sunburn, and dehydration can be major problems. Drink a lot of water and stay out of the sun.

Respect the sea. The Mediterranean is calm, but has a deceptively strong undercurrent. Over 100 people drown each year in Israel.

Dress modestly. In Tel Aviv anything goes, but in Jerusalem cover up if you want to be allowed into the holy sites.

Eat Mediterranean fast food. Not McDonalds but falafel stuffed into pita bread, with as much salad as you can eat. Healthy, cheap, and tasty.

Practice your bargaining skills. Never pay the first price quoted to you in Jerusalem's Old City markets.

Smear your body with Dead Sea mud. The Dead Sea is rich in minerals. Smearing yourself with mud may make you look ridiculous, but your skin will glow afterward.

Hire a bike. Tel Aviv has 150km (93 miles) of bicycle lanes, including along the seafront. The Tel-O-Fun municipal bike rental program, easily identified by their bright green color, is set to be introduced in Jerusalem in 2020.

Remember the Holocaust. A visit to the Yad Vashem Holocaust Museum in Jerusalem is fundamental to understanding the recent history that shaped Israel.

Visit a kibbutz. The farming collectives that helped build Israel are mainly in rural areas, but there are many between Tel Aviv and Jerusalem with guesthouses.

Travel by train. Forget about the new Tel Aviv–Jerusalem fast rail link. Take the old Ottoman railroad through the Jerusalem hills via Beit Shemesh. It's slower but much more scenic.

See Israel in miniature. Mini-Israel, located between Jerusalem and Tel Aviv near the airport, is a great way of whetting your appetite for the country's iconic sites, or even summing them up after you've seen them.

Rav-Kav multiride ticket. Buy a Rav-Kav multiride ticket at one of the central bus or train stations. The tickets are good for all buses, trains, and the Jerusalem light rail, and are a more economical way of traveling around Jerusalem and Tel Aviv than taxi or rented car.

Israeli salad and hummus

FOOD AND DRINK

Variety is the spice of life, and Israeli food brings the culinary traditions of Diaspora Jews together, with the added ingredient of the country's innovation. Rich in spices and diversity, Mediterranean and Middle Eastern cuisine is both tasty and healthy.

This is the region where farming first developed around 9500 BC. Today there remains a delight, sophistication, and creativity about the region's food that has only been enhanced through the ages. Most of the founder crops of the Levant remain influential in today's cooking – wheat, barley, peas, lentils, chickpeas, flax, and vetch – as do the seven species of Jewish tradition: wheat barley, dates, figs, grapes, olives, and pomegranates. Rearing livestock, mainly sheep and goats, for food was also introduced in the region. This was the biblical land, flowing with milk and honey, although milk was mainly from the sheep and goats, and the honey was actually dates.

The predominant food style in Israel reflects the country's geographical location, overlapping the Mediterranean and the Middle East. The heavier, less healthy meat dishes brought to Israel from Europe by Ashkenazi Jews can still be found, but have for the most part made way for the healthier, spicier foods of Sephardi Jews from the Middle East.

Each Jewish ethnic group, whether Moroccan, Libyan, Tunisian, Yemenite, Iraqi, or native-born (Sabra) Israeli, has its own special dish and its own holiday fare. Their foods are similar in some ways, yet quite distinct in others. Basic herbs and spices include cumin, fresh and dried coriander, mint, garlic, onion, turmeric, black pepper, *za'atar* (an oregano-based spice mixture), cardamom, and fresh green chilli. Dark, fruity olive oil adds further fragrance.

LOCAL CUISINE

Arab food is similar and both Arab and Sephardi Jewish meals traditionally begin the same way – with a variety of savoury mezze salads. Hummus – ground chickpea seasoned with tahini (sesame paste), lemon juice, garlic, and cumin – is probably the most popular dip, spread, and salad rolled into one. You'll also find the most astounding variety of egg-

Fresh olives   *Bread and bagels*

plant salads you've ever seen: eggplant in tahini, fried sliced eggplant, chopped eggplant with vegetable, and many more. Tabbouleh, which is made from finely chopped parsley, tomatoes, mint, onion, bulgur, and seasoned with olive oil, lemon juice, salt and pepper, is another popular mezze dish. Assorted pickled vegetables are generally considered salads in Israel.

Waiters may show some signs of disappointment, but you can order a selection of these salads as a meal in themselves, usually for about $15. Or you may follow them with a kebab (grilled, ground spiced meat), *shishlik* (grilled, sliced lamb or beef with lamb fat), *seniya* (beef or lamb in tahini sauce), or stuffed chicken.

The main types of fish available in Israel are trout, grey and red mullet, sea bass, bream, and the local specialty St Peter's fish (*tilapia*) – generally served fried or grilled, sometimes accompanied by a piquant sauce. Authentic North African restaurants will also feature *harimeh* – hot and spicy cooked fish, fragrant with an appetizing blend of tomatoes, cumin and hot pepper.

For dessert, in Arab restaurants this may mean *baklava* (filo pastry sprinkled with nuts and sweet syrup), other rich sweets, or fruit. In Sephardi Jewish restaurants this could mean crème caramel custard, chocolate mousse or an egg-white confection laced with chocolate syrup and called (for some unknown reason) Bavarian cream. Turkish coffee or tea with fresh mint ends the meal. If you do not want sugar in your coffee, tell the waiter in advance, or your drink will be liberally sweetened.

EATING KOSHER

The laws of *kashrut* are extremely complex, but in practical terms they mean that many animals, most notably the pig, cannot be eaten at all. Furthermore, kosher animals such as the cow and chicken must be killed in a specific way – by having their throats cut – otherwise the meat is not considered kosher.

The blood must also be drained out of kosher meat, often making a steak, for example, somewhat desiccated and lacking in flavor.

In addition, while most fish are permissible, all seafood (shrimp, lobsters, octopus, etc.) is considered unclean. Finally, meat and milk cannot be consumed together at the same meal.

This said, many secular Jews disregard dietary laws, and most restaurants in Israel, especially those outside Jerusalem, are not kosher. Outside of hotels, all kosher restaurants are closed on the Jewish festivals and the Sabbath, from sunset on Friday through to sunset on Saturday.

WHERE TO EAT

The ultimate Israeli snack or light meal has to be falafel (fried chickpea balls served in pita bread, with a wide variety of vegetables). Along the sidewalks of major streets you can usually find several adjoining falafel stands where you're free

Fresh fruit for sale

to stuff your pita with salads and pickles for as long as the bread holds out. Another popular chickpea snack is hummus, a paste from ground chickpea mopped up by pita and served with olive oil, beans, mushrooms and a range of other options.

Tel Aviv's Carmel Market and the adjoining Kerem Hatamanim, together with Jerusalem's Makhanei Yehuda market and the neighboring Agrippas Street are the most famous centers for these snacks, but most city streets have similar eateries that will also offer shawarma, turkey or chicken carved from a spit like a gyro kebab.

These areas have more upscale restaurants too, but the most expensive traditional restaurants tend to be in hotels. Downtown Jerusalem and Mamilla also have many restaurants, almost all of them kosher, while Tel Aviv's restaurants are spread throughout the city from the port in the north, to Jaffa in the south. The city also has a more innovative and sophisticated tradition, with the many such high-end restaurants around Rothschild Boulevard or near the Sarona food market.

Other street food favorites include bagel-shaped sesame-sprinkled breads (served with *za'atar*), nuts, and sunflower seeds. Also popular are *bourekas*, a small savoury pastry stuffed with cheese, potatoes, mushrooms and spinach. Pizza, blintzes, waffles, and burgers are imported staples that are widely available.

Fruit and Vegetables

A trip to the open-air Makhanei Yehuda in Jerusalem or the Carmel market in Tel Aviv will reveal a sumptuous array of fruit and vegetables, featuring everything from apples to artichokes, kohlrabi to celeriac. Subtropical fruits include kiwi, mango, persimmon, loquat, passion fruit, *chirimoya*, and papaya. Fresh dates, figs, pomegranates, and the world's largest strawberries (in winter only) are among the seasonal treats.

Meat

If you like fowl and game, you will find chicken and turkey and, in more up-scale restaurants, goose and duck make excellent choices. While much beef is imported, all fowl is domestically raised.

Cheese and Milk

In biblical times water was scarce and unpalatable, so milk became a major component of the diet. Goat's milk was the richest and most nourishing; next came that of sheep, then cow's milk, and finally milk from a camel. Today's Israel continues the 'land of milk and honey' tradition, with a wealth of familiar cheeses (camembert, brie, cottage, and Gouda), together with a wide variety of goat and sheep yogurt, all readily available.

Breads

Pita bread has a pocket for tucking in meat, salad, and falafel while *lafa is* a flatbread from Iraq that's wrapped around whatever contents come to hand. In Yemeni restaurants several types of bread are served: *mallawah* (crispy fried, fattening and delicious);

Cheese shop

lahuh (light, pancake-like); and *jahnoon* (slow-baked strudel-like dough). Otherwise all the standard breads are available, from sliced plain white to delicious French baguettes.

DRINK

Soft Drinks

Israel's warm weather means tourists need to take in large amounts of liquid so it is best stick to water most of the time. Tap water is healthy, while bottled mineral water is widely available. There is the usual range of Coca Cola and other sweetened drinks and juices available, as well as much healthier freshly squeezed fruit juices. For a few dollars, street vendors will squeeze you an orange, carrot, grapefruit, kiwi, or a dozen other fruit drinks.

Coffee and Tea

Israelis take their coffee seriously. Most popular are Middle Eastern coffee (*botz*), Bedouin coffee (*botz* with cardamom), Turkish coffee, Viennese coffee (*café hafuch*), espresso and Americano. Turkish and Middle Eastern coffee can be very small and very strong. If you are thirsty, and not just in need of a caffeine hit, order a glass of iced water with it. Remember to tell the waiter when you order if you don't want your coffee with sugar. Don't expect strong English tea with milk anywhere, but most restaurants give a good choice of herbal teas that are served without milk.

Alcohol

Quality wines have been developed in Israel, pushing aside the sweet red wines traditionally preferred for religious occasions. Israeli wine growers have discovered that viticulture is a skill best practiced in the cooler inland hills, with state-of-the-art wineries importing know-how and the finest vine stock from France, California, and Australia. Several local beers, both bottled and draught, and a range of imported beers, are readily available. There are both home-distilled and imported spirits and liquors too, including the local specialty *arak*, similar to Greece's *ouzo*.

Generally speaking, cafés and restaurants in Arab locations throughout Israel do not serve alcohol.

Vegan paradise

Israel is one of the world's major centers of vegan cuisine (abstaining from meat, fish, dairy and eggs). Few cities have more vegan restaurants than Tel Aviv and many eateries have vegan options – the city has some 400 vegan or vegan-friendly restaurants. Kosher food separates meat and dairy, so vegans can be sure that dishes in a kosher meat restaurant can be guaranteed not to have any dairy items. Middle Eastern fare is also very creative with plant-based foods and the mezze, savoury salads served at the start of the meal (hummus, tahini etc), is completely vegan.

Jerusalem's Old City market

SHOPPING

Israel's malls may be air-conditioned havens from the heat, but high prices are a deterrent. However, the county's many markets will capture your imagination, from the bazaars of Jerusalem's Old City, to Tel Aviv's Carmel market.

Although the country has excellent shopping malls, Israel's cost of living is relatively high, so it is advisable to restrict purchases of routine consumer goods and clothes. For the most part, overseas shoppers will be hunting for souvenirs or items that are unique to Israel, including exclusive jewelry, diamonds, oriental carpets, antiquities, paintings, sculptures, silverware, and, of course, religious items, particularly Judaica and Christian icons.

Stores in malls and city centers are dominated by retail chains including international fashion outlets such as Forever 21, American Eagle, and GAP. Stores tend to open long hours, usually 9am–9pm Sunday to Thursday with most stores closed on Friday afternoons and Saturday during the day for Sabbath, as well as on Jewish holidays. Israel has excellent shopping malls, which can provide an air-conditioned oasis during the heat of the day. But the real treat for tourists is the country's colorful markets.

JERUSALEM

When buying souvenirs from the Holy City, visitors may want to visit the Mamilla Shopping Mall, a strip mall linking Downtown Jerusalem with the Jaffa Gate. Be aware, however, that prices here are among the most expensive in Israel. The city's largest shopping center – Malka Shopping Mall – is well out of the city center and can only be reached by car, taxi, or bus.

Centers for buying fine crafts, jewelry and Judaica include the House of Quality, Khutsot ha-Yoster (Arts and Crafts Lane), and the Me'a She'arim neighborhood. The latter is the best place to get a bargain, while King David Street has the exclusive, high-end antiques and Judaica stores.

Jerusalem Markets

The Old City market in the Muslim Quarter is a delightful oriental bazaar. Straight through from the Jaffa Gate you'll find dozens of small stores with all the souvenirs, religious icons, leather goods, and bric-a-brac that you could ever want. You will have to bargain with the shopkeepers, though. Don't be afraid to walk away. In fact, it can be a useful method: you'll know that the shopkeeper has reached the low-

Souvenirs, Carmel Market

Dizengoff Center, Tel Aviv

est price they are willing to sell at if they don't call you back. Makhanei Yehuda market, in downtown Jerusalem, is the place to go for foodies. Expect fresh produce, spices, pickles, nuts, coffee and a lot more.

TEL AVIV

Escaping to an air-conditioned shopping mall can be even more pleasant in Tel Aviv, with its heat and humidity. Try the Azrieli Shopping Center, located by Haohalom train station, or the Dizengoff Center, by Dizengoff Square. Opposite the Azrieli Center is the Sarona Market, which includes an indoor food market and an outdoor mall, set attractively among the 19th-century buildings of Tel Aviv's German Colony. Israel is one of the diamond capitals of the world; goods deals are available at the Ramat Gan Diamond Exchange and throughout the city.

Tel Aviv Markets

The city has excellent markets including the Carmel Market for fresh produce and food in general, the Bezalel Market for clothes, Levinsky Market for spices, nuts, dried fruit and coffee, the Nahlat Binyamin market for arts and crafts (Tuesdays and Fridays only), and the Jaffa flea market for antiques. Also Tel Aviv's port has a farmers' market on weekends for gourmet cheeses and high-quality, fresh produce.

SALES TAX

After your passport has been stamped for exit, you can apply to the bank in the airport departure hall for a 17 percent VAT (value-added tax) refund on selected purchases over 400 shekels (roughly $110). You cannot claim a refund for any food or drink and only purchases made from stores participating in the 'tax refund for tourists' scheme are eligible (look for a sticker in the window). You must ensure that the total net sum (after the 17 percent reduction) on one invoice is more than $50, and present valid tax-refund receipts for your purchases, not just ordinary receipts.

Ben Gurion Airport has a duty-free store with the usual selection of alcohol, gifts and fashion brands. However, despite the lower taxes, goods are usually cheaper in regular stores around the country. As with all international airports, stores know they have a captive audience with time to kill and gifts to buy.

It is forbidden to export antiquities from Israel unless you obtain a written export permit from the Department of Antiquities and Museums. A 10 percent export fee is payable on the purchase price of every item approved for export. For more details, contact the Department of Antiquities and Museums, Rockefeller Museum, opposite Herod's Gate, POB 586, Jerusalem, tel: (02) 627 8627.

Celebrating Purim in Me'a She'arim, Jerusalem

RELIGIOUS FESTIVALS & HOLIDAYS

With religion playing such a major role in Israeli life, especially in Jerusalem, you should be aware of the major Jewish, Christian, and Muslim holidays, as the celebrations that can enhance your visit, or disrupt your schedule.

Barely a week goes by in Israel without a religious holiday. While this has a major impact on the cycle of life in pious Jerusalem, Jewish holidays are public holidays and in secular Tel Aviv, many residents go to the beach or a café, rather than the synagogue.

Knowing when a religious holiday is likely to fall is a complicated business though: Jews and Muslims have their own calendars, while the Western churches follow the familiar Gregorian calendar and the Orthodox churches calculate holidays according to the Julian calendar.

JEWISH HOLIDAYS

The Jewish calendar is a solar-lunar calendar, with a leap month added every two to three years, so that festivals continue to fall (roughly) the same time in the solar year. Consequently, exact dates and even exact months in the Gregorian calendar cannot be given. Jewish holidays, like the Sabbath, begin and end at sunset.

January/February

Tu B'Shvat – New Year for Trees. Tree-planting takes place to encourage the forestation of the country.

March/April

Purim – Celebrating the saving of Persian Jews. Fancy dress is worn and there is a carnival-like atmosphere.

Passover – Seven-day festival celebrating the Jewish exodus from Egypt. The first and last days are public holidays; Jews don't eat bread throughout.

April/May

Holocaust Day – A day dedicated to the memory of those murdered in the Holocaust. Places of entertainment are closed.

Memorial Day – On the eve of Independence Day, dedicated to soldiers killed in action and victims of terror. Places of entertainment are closed.

Independence Day – Marks Israel's Declaration of Independence in 1948.

Lag B'Omer – A Jewish bonfire night of sorts celebrating the life of Rabbi Shimon bar Yochai, a Mishnaic sage from the 2nd century.

May/June

Shavuot (Pentecost) – 50 days after Passover this festival, which is also a public holiday, marks the giving of the Torah to Moses, and is also a harvest festival.

Good Friday procession on Via Dolorosa

July/August
Tisha B'Av – Commemorating the destruction of both Temples. Places of entertainment are closed. Jews traditionally fast on this day.

September/October
Rosh Hashana – Jewish New Year (two days)
Yom Kippur – No vehicles travel on the roads. Jews traditionally fast on this day
Sukkot – Jews build tabernacles (temporary gazebo-like tents) to remind themselves of the 40 years they spent in the desert after leaving Egypt.

November/December
Hanukkah – The eight-day festival of lights recalls the Jewish victory over the Greeks.

MUSLIM HOLIDAYS

The Muslim calendar is completely lunar, with 12 months comprising a year, so each Muslim year is 354 or 355 days. Thus, the month of Ramadan rotates backwards through the year and can fall in any season. Muslim festivals, therefore, cannot be attributed to any single Gregorian month.

However, the most important Muslim holidays are:
Id el Adha – Sacrificial Festival.
New Year.
Mohammed's Birthday.
Feast of Ramadan (one month of fasting from sunrise to sunset).
Id el Fitr – conclusion of Ramadan.

CHRISTIAN HOLIDAYS

Western churches use the Gregorian calendar, while Orthodox churches use the Julian calendar. Christmas, and sometimes Easter, are celebrated on different dates to Western Churches.

January
January 6/7 – Orthodox Christmas Eve and Christmas Day.
January 19 – Armenian Orthodox Christmas.

March/April
Easter – Western Churches – The first weekend after the first full moon after the vernal equinox, usually immediately after the Jewish Passover.
Easter – Orthodox Churches – Often celebrated later due to the Julian calendar. On Good Friday, processions are held in Jerusalem, where Christ was crucified, buried and resurrected.

May/June
Whitsun/Pentecost – Celebrated seven weeks after Easter, commemorates the coming of the Holy Spirit to the disciples following the death of Jesus Christ.

December 24/25
Christmas – The Catholic and Protestant Churches celebrate the birth of Christ. The place to be is Bethlehem in the Palestinian Territories just south of Jerusalem, where it is believed Christ was born.

The Israel Philharmonic Orchestra

ENTERTAINMENT

Israelis work hard and play hard. Both Jerusalem and Tel Aviv offer much to do at night, ranging from music, dance, and theater, to a diverse range of arts festivals, and of course a lively nightlife scene.

Tel Aviv bills itself as Israel's cultural capital, and is home to the lion's share of performing art, with the nation's premiere music, dance, and theater companies, as well as performances from overseas visiting stars. It is also the city that never stops, with bars and clubs offering a diverse range of live music, often packed with revelers well into the early hours of the morning.

Jerusalem, despite being the Holy City, is not as prim as you might expect. Here too, you will find many theaters, music companies, and regular appearances by other nationwide acts. Jerusalem's nightlife is also surprising lively, with much of the city center bustling after dark.

MUSIC

There are several Israeli orchestras, of which the most famous is the Israel Philharmonic, playing under the baton of the great conductors of the world. The Jerusalem Symphony Orchestra gives weekly concerts in Jerusalem in the winter season. Israel also has its own opera company.

Mann Auditorium (for Israel Symphony Orchestra), 1 Huberman, Tel Aviv. Tel: (03) 621 1777. www.hatarbut.co.il

Israel Opera House, Sha'ul ha-Melekh Boulevard. Tel: (03) 692 7777. www.israel-opera.co.il

Henry Crown Hall (for Jerusalem Symphony Orchestra), Marcus, Jerusalem. Tel: 1-700-70-4000. www.jso.co.il

At the other end of the market, many bars offer live music and cover bands. Molly Bloom's in Tel Aviv offers live Israeli bands playing Irish music with Hebrew lyrics. Also Sultan's Pool Ampitheater, located beneath the walls of the Old City, is a great venue for live music..

DANCE

Professional dance companies include the Israel Classical Ballet, the Batsheva Dance Company, the Bat-Dor Dance Company, Kol Hademana, and the Kibbutz Dance Company. Batsheva and Bat-Dor are both modern dance groups. All dance groups perform regularly in Jerusalem and Tel Aviv.

Suzan Dalal Center, 6 Yekhi'el, Neve Tsedek, Tel Aviv. Tel: (03) 517 1471. For Batsheva and Inbal Dance Troupes, Israel Ballet Tel: (03) 696 6610.

Kibbutz Contemporary Dance Co. Tel: (03) 692 5278.

Jerusalem Dance Theater Tel: (02) 679 5626.

Batsheva Dance Company *Tel Aviv's Jerusalem beach on a Friday night*

THEATER

Theater is very popular in Israel, and there are many companies performing a wide range of classical and contemporary plays in Hebrew, including original works by Israelis, with simultaneous translations often available. The best-known are the Habima and Carmeri theaters in Tel Aviv. In Jerusalem, there is the Jerusalem Theater, the Henry Crown Auditorium, and the Rebecca Crown Theater. Smaller companies offer stage productions in English, Yiddish, and other languages.

Jerusalem Theater, Marcus, Jerusalem. Tel: (02) 561 0011/561 0293.

Habima Theater, Tarsith Boulevard, Tel Aviv. Tel: (03) 526 6666.

Carmeri Theater, 101 Dizengoff, Tel Aviv. Tel: (03) 523 3335.

MOVIES

There are multiplex movie theaters in all Israel's major cities and for about $10 you can see the latest Hollywood offerings. You'll also find the latest movies from France, Germany and elsewhere, usually with English subtitles, but ask at the box office first if unsure. Israel itself produces a dozen or so films each year, which offer an insight into local culture. These, too, have English subtitles. Local cinematheques show golden oldies, as well the more recent offerings.

Jerusalem Cinematheque, Derekh Hevron. Tel: (02) 565 4333. www.jer-cin.org.il

Tel Aviv Cinematheque, 2 Sprintzach. Tel: (03) 693 8111. www.cinema.co.il/en/

NIGHTLIFE

Nightlife starts late in Israel and is very vibrant. From 10pm onward, Israelis begin to pack the streets of Tel Aviv, Jerusalem, and most other Israeli cities. Street-side cafés and restaurants are busy until well after midnight, while bars and discos have a brisk trade right through the night. The Israeli weekend is comprised of Friday and Saturday, so Thursday night is a big night out.

Tel Aviv seafront and other hotspots are often crowded throughout the night. Nightclubs abound in the main cities and resort towns. Rock, jazz, folk, and pop music are the usual fare for live music, with Jerusalem and Tel Aviv the best places to catch a live performance. The bohemian Florontin is another popular nightspot in Tel Aviv, as well as the newly renovated Tel Aviv Port and Old Jaffa Port.

Although lower-profile than that of Tel Aviv's, Jerusalem's nightlife is certainly vibrant, especially between April and October, when it is warm enough to stroll through the streets and sit outside at cafés and restaurants. The city's nightlife, as elsewhere in Israel, really gets going after 10pm and the streets remain packed until well after midnight. The focus of Jerusalem's nightlife is the Mahane Yehuda market and surrounding streets, the Russian Compound, and the eastern end of Jaffa Road.

HISTORY: KEY DATES

Archeological evidence suggests that farming evolved in this region some 12,000 years ago and there are remains of human settlements on the Mediterranean coast, Judean Desert and Jordan Valley.

10,000 BC	Some of the world's first farming settlements are established in Israel.
3000 BC	Canaanite city kingdoms develop based on Mesopotamia–Egypt trade.

THE BIBLICAL PERIOD

2000 BC	Abraham moves from Mesopotamia to Be'er Sheva.
1280 BC	Moses leads the Israelites out of Egypt toward Canaan.
1225 BC	Joshua catches Jericho.
1000 BC	King David builds Jerusalem as his capital.
950 BC	King Solomon builds the First Temple.
605 BC	The Babylonians conquer Jerusalem and destroy the First Temple.
520 BC	Jews return to Jerusalem from the Babylonian exile and build the Second Temple.
63 BC	The Romans conquer Judea, and in the following decades destroy the Second Temple, and exile the Jews.
37BC	King Herod assumes the throne, founds Caesarea, and rebuilds the Second Temple.

THE CHRISTIAN AND MUSLIM ERAS

30	Jesus Christ is crucified.
66	The Jews revolt against Rome.
132	Bar Kochba's revolt against the Romans fails, and most of the Jews go into exile. The Romans recapture Jerusalem and destroy the Temple.
325	Roman Emperor Constantine converts to Christianity and sends his mother to the Holy Land to identify the sacred sites.
637	The Muslims capture Jerusalem and build the Dome of the Rock on the Temple Mount.

Israeli flags flying in the wind on Independence Day

CRUSADERS, MAMELUKES AND OTTOMANS

1099	The Crusaders capture the Holy Land.
1291	The Mamelukes defeat the Crusaders in Akko and take full control of Palestine.
1516	The Ottoman Turks capture Palestine and Suleiman the Magnificent builds the walls around Jerusalem.
1799	Napoleon occupies part of the Holy Land.

THE BIRTH OF ZIONISM

1878	The first Zionist settlements are established.
1917	The British become the rulers of Palestine after defeating the Ottomans, issuing the Balfour Declaration that states Palestine should become a Jewish State.
1925	Large-scale Jewish immigration from Europe begins.
1939–45	Six million Jews are murdered in the Holocaust.

INDEPENDENT ISRAEL

1948	Israel declares independence.
1967	Israel captures the West Bank, Gaza, Sinai, and Golan Heights during the Six Day War.
1973	The Yom Kippur War.
1977	29 years of Labor Party rule end as the right-wing Likud wins power, signs a peace treaty with Egypt, and accelerates the building of Jewish settlements in the West Bank.
1987	The First Intifada begins.
1995	Prime Minister Yitzhak Rabin is assassinated in Tel Aviv.
2000	Peace talks with the Palestinians break down and the Second Intifada begins.
2005	Israel withdraws from Gaza.
2015	Benjamin Netanyahu elected for a fourth term as prime minister.
2017	US President Donald Trump announces that America officially recognises Jerusalem as the capital of Israel and will move its embassy there, reigniting tensions in the region.
2018	Israeli forces and Hamas clash in Gaza after a covert operation goes wrong, and an Israeli officer is killed.

BEST ROUTES

JERUSALEM'S OLD CITY

Sacred to Jews, Christians and Muslims, within the walls of the Old City are the remains of the Second Jewish Temple, the site of Christ's crucifixion and resurrection, and the Dome of the Rock, from where Mohammed ascended to heaven.

DISTANCE: 3km (1.9 miles)
TIME: A full day
START: Jaffa Gate
END: Zion Gate
POINTS TO NOTE: Dress modestly when visiting the holy sites. When purchasing items in the Old City market, storekeepers will always ask for inflated prices first – it is customary for the buyer to bargain.

The Old City houses the most sacred shrines to Judaism, Christianity and Islam, a bustling market, and is divided into Jewish, Christian, Armenian, and Muslim quarters. Less than a square kilometer in size, the Old City is encircled by walls built by Ottoman ruler Suleiman the Magnificent in 1541. The walls protect the world's most intensely coveted real estate, which has been fought over for centuries by invaders. Yet there is more harmony in the Old City than you might expect, with the practical need to encourage tourism and provide a livelihood for its residents prevailing over national and religious jealousies and zealousness.

JAFFA GATE

The main entrance to the Old City is the **Jaffa Gate ❶**. To the right of the Jaffa Gate is a vehicle entrance, which is the widest gap in the Old City walls. It is here that the city walls were breached at the end of the 19th century to allow Kaiser Wilhelm of Prussia and his vehicle escort to enter. Once inside the city walls, you'll see the **Municipal Tourist Information Office** (Sun–Thu 8.30am–5pm). Also nearby is the **Christian Information Office** (Mon–Fri 8.30am–5.30pm, Sat 8.30am–12.30pm).

Muslim Quarter Market

Just in from the Jaffa Gate is the entrance to the **Muslim Quarter Souk (Bazaar) ❷**, where friendly shopkeepers will assault you with trinkets at 'special prices'. Be sure to bargain with them. At the end of the Bazaar, just before the T-junction, turn right onto Ha-Kardo and proceed to the Jewish Quarter.

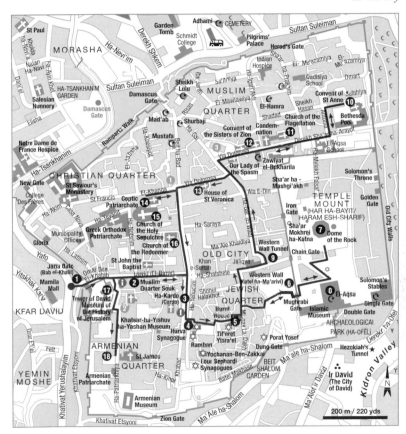

Jewish Quarter

Large parts of the Jewish Quarter were rebuilt after the reunification of Jerusalem following the Six-Day War in 1967. **Ha-Kardo ❸**, the main route into the Jewish Quarter, is a submerged pedestrian byway that was the main north–south axis built by the Romans in AD 70. Nearby is the great **Hurva Synagogue ❹**, which was rebuilt in original 19th-century neo-Byzantine style and reopened in 2010. At the end of Tif'eret

Yisra'el is a fascinating archeological site, the **Burnt House** ❺ (Sun–Thu 9am–5pm, Fri 9am–1pm), which was the residence of the priestly Bar-Kathros clan during the Jewish revolt against Rome, from AD 66–73.

THE WESTERN WALL

The steps at the end of Tif'eret Yisra'el lead down to the most important site in Judaism: the **Western Wall** ❻ (always open; free). A retaining wall for the western side of the Temple Mount, constructed from massive carved stone blocks from the Herodian era, the Western Wall is the only remnant of the Second Temple complex to survive demolition by the Romans, and has inspired Jews for 2,000 years.

The area in front of the wall is divided into separate sections for male and female prayer. Non-Orthodox Jewish women often challenge the status-quo by bringing Torah scrolls into the female side, antagonizing the local rabbinate.

THE TEMPLE MOUNT

Behind the Western Wall, reached by an entrance to the right, is the **Temple Mount** (Sun–Thu 7.30–11.30am and 12.30–1.30pm; during Ramadan, Fri and other Muslim holidays closed to non-Muslims; free), which Muslims call **Haram esh-Sharif** (meaning the Venerable Sanctuary). This is the biblical Mount Moriah where Abraham nearly sacrificed Isaac, where the First and Second Temples once stood, and where the golden **Dome of the Rock** and the silver-domed **El-Aqsa Mosque** now stand.

The Temple Mount is Jerusalem's most disputed land, and lies at the heart of the Israel-Palestinian conflict. The Arab nations are determined that an Islamic flag must fly over the site. Israel leaves administration of Haram esh-Sharif entirely to Muslim officials called the Waqf. However, Israeli Border Police do provide security, in cooperation with Arab police officers. Israel's Chief Rabbinate has banned Jews from visiting the Temple

Ramparts Walk

From the Jaffa Gate you can access the **Ramparts Walk** (daily 9am–4pm). This walk takes you around the top of the city walls and provides marvellous views of the Old City rooftops and the new city. On a clear winter day, you can see the hills surrounding the city too. The walk is divided into two parts, each going in an opposite directions: from Jaffa Gate to the Dung Gate near the Western Wall and Temple Mount; and from Jaffa Gate via the Damascus Gate to Lions Gate at the start of Via Dolorosa. It is possible to exit at any of the gates rather than retracing your steps but you can only pay and enter at the Jaffa Gate. The ticket (which costs 8 shekels, roughly $2) is valid for two days so you don't have to attempt both walks on the same day.

The Dome of the Rock

Mount as it is believed that somewhere on the hill is the site of the ancient Holy of Holies, the inner sanctuary that only the High Priest was allowed to enter. However, many nationalist Israelic provocatively hold prayer services on the Mount.

Dome of the Rock and El-Aqsa Mosque

The most eye-catching structure on Haram esh-Sharif is the **Dome of the Rock ❼**. The outside of the edifice, which is a shrine and not a mosque, is a fantasia of marble, mosaics, stained glass, painted tiles, and quotations from the Koran, all capped by the gold-plated aluminium dome.

The inside of the Dome of the Rock focuses on the huge boulder called the **Kubbet es-Sakhra**, the sacred rock on which Abraham was said to have prepared the sacrifice of Isaac. It is also the spot on which, during his mystical journey to Jerusalem, Mohammed is said to have mounted his steed and ascended to heaven. Since 2000, non-Muslims have not been permitted to visit the interiors of the Dome of the Rock or the El-Aqsa Mosque.

The silver-capped mosque to the south is **El-Aqsa ❽**. Able to accommodate 5,000 worshippers, El-Aqsa has a functional design and straddles vast underground chambers known as **Solomon's Stables**.

Western Wall Tunnels

Back down by the Western Wall is the entrance to the **Western Wall Tunnels ❾** (Sun–Thu 7.20am–late, Fri 7.20am–noon; advance reservation is necessary, tel: 9722 627 1333). Archeologists have excavated a 2,000-year-old street leading along the rim of the Temple Mount, several hundred meters northward to the Via Dolorosa.

If you cannot arrange a tour through the tunnels, ascend the steps facing westward to the right of the Western Wall plaza and turn right into the Ha-Gai (Al Wad) alleyway. Several hundred meters along on the right is the Via Dolorosa. Walk down to the end, in order to start at the First Station.

VIA DOLOROSA

The **Via Dolorosa**, the most sacred route in Christendom, marks Christ's journey to his crucifixion, burial, and resurrection. Begin at the **Convent of St Anne ❿**, just inside from St Stephen's Gate (Lions Gate), the best-preserved Crusader church in the Holy Land, with a crypt designated as Mary's birthplace.

The **First Station of the Cross**, where Jesus was sentenced, is to the left, inside the courtyard of the Umariyah school. The **Second Station**, where Jesus received the Cross, is opposite, on the street outside the **Chapel of Condemnation** and the **Church of the Flagellation ⓫**. It was here that Jesus was scourged and had the crown of thorns placed on his head.

In the nearby **Convent of the Sisters of Zion ⓬** is a huge underground chamber called the **Lithostrotos** (Mon–Sat

Station 6, on Via Dolorosa

8.30am–12.30pm, 2–4.30pm), said to be where Pontius Pilate judged Jesus. Continue up Via Dolorosa, and turn left when it traverses El Wad ha-Gai.

On the corner of El Wad ha-Gai and Via Dolorosa, you'll find the **Austrian Hospice Viennese Café ❶**, a great spot to escape from the hustle and bustle of the busy streets of the Old City.

Continue down Via Dolorosa, and you'll see the **Third Station** on the right, where Jesus fell with the Cross, which is commemorated by a column in a wall. Next door is the **Fourth Station**, where Jesus encountered Mary. On this site is the **Armenian Catholic Church of Our Lady of the Spasm**.

For a lighter lunch try **Abu Shukri ❷**, a little farther down on the left. At this point, Via Dolorosa becomes a steep lane ascending to the right from El Wad ha-Gai, opposite Abu Shukri. The nearby **Fifth Station** is where Simon the Cyrenian helped Jesus carry the Cross. The **Sixth Station**, at the **House of St Veronica ⓭**, is where Veronica cleansed the face of Jesus. Where Via Dolorosa bisects the souk's Khan ez-Zeit Bazaar is the **Seventh Station**, where Jesus fell again.

The Church of the Holy Sepulchre and the last Stations of the Cross are close by. The **Eighth Station** is outside the **Greek Orthodox Chapel of St Charalampos**, and at the **Coptic Patriarchate ⓮** compound, off the Khan ez-Zeit Bazaar, a pillar marks the **Ninth Station**, where Jesus stumbled for the third time.

THE CHURCH OF THE HOLY SEPULCHRE

The **Church of the Holy Sepulchre ⓯** (daily, dawn–dusk; free) was built by the Crusaders in the 12th century, and added to over the centuries. Several Christian communities share the church, and are responsible for scrupulously specified areas. Church fathers have battled over who cleans which steps. With its gloomy interior, its competing chants and multiple aromas of incense, the church exudes magnificence. The focal points are the hillock where the Crucifixion took place (Golgotha in Hebrew, or Calvary in Latin), and Christ's tomb.

Stairs to the right inside the door to the church lead up to **Calvary**. The **Tenth Station**, where Jesus was stripped of his garments, is marked by a floor mosaic. The next three stations are located at Latin and Greek altars on this same level, within a few paces of each other. They mark the nailing of Jesus to the Cross, the placing of the Cross, and the removal of Christ's body. The **Fourteenth Station** is below the Holy Sepulchre; Christ's tomb is downstairs under the church's main rotunda.

Church of the Redeemer

The tower of the **Lutheran Church of the Redeemer ⓰** (Mon–Sat 9am–5pm) is the highest point in the Old City, offering a magnificent view. To get there from the Church of the Holy Sepulchre, follow the main thorough-

Church of the Holy Sepulchre

The Tower of David Museum

fare out of the Damascus Gate, turn left and uphill, toward Jaffa Gate.

Tower of David Museum

Return to the Jaffa Gate and turn right before the souk. To your right, inside the Citadel, is the **Tower of David Museum of the History of Jerusalem** ⓱ (Sun–Thu 10am–4pm, in summer until 5pm and 10pm on Sun, Sat 10am–2pm), which was once a medieval fortress.

The museum contains displays describing the tumultuous history of the city, a 19th-century model of the Old City, and the multi-layered ruins of the structure itself. Visit in the evening for a multimedia show, where the walls themselves are the palette for the sound and light show. For more info, call 02-626 5333 or visit www.towerofdavid.org.il.

The Armenian Quarter

Outside the museum, continue right along the narrow road to the **Armenian Quarter** ⓲ (Mon–Fri 6.30–7.30am and 3–3.40pm and Sat–Sun 6.30–9.30am), a walled enclave within a walled city. A modest doorway leads to the 12th-century **St James's Cathedral**, one of the most impressive churches in the Old City. Continue along the road and exit the Old City at the Zion Gate, or retrace your steps a little for an early dinner at the **Armenian Tavern** ❸.

Food and Drink

❶ AUSTRIAN HOSPICE VIENNESE CAFÉ

37 Via Dolorosa; tel: 02-626 5800; daily 10am–10pm; $$

Although this café is located firmly in the Middle East, the decor, atmosphere, and the menu will take you back in time to 19th-century Vienna, with the apple strudel making this an ideal stop-off for afternoon tea. Dinner is also served here, with schnitzel and goulash being the house specialties.

❷ ABU SHUKRI

63 Al Wad Road (Via Dolorosa); tel: 02-627 1538; daily 8am–4.30pm, later in summer and Sat; $

Famous for serving the best hummus in the Old City, Abu Shukri is perfect for a light lunch. Located in the Muslim quarter on Via Dolorosa, it offers straightforward tasty, smooth hummus with various toppings, including tahini, fava beans, and pine nuts, as well as falafel at very reasonable prices.

❸ ARMENIAN TAVERN

79 Armenian Orthodox Patriarchate Road; tel: 02-627 3854; Mon–Sat noon–10pm; $$

This restaurant's authentic Armenian cuisine is enhanced by its location in an historic Crusader building, and its atmosphere is complemented by the background Greek and Armenian music. The appetizers are filling, and the main courses are comprised mainly of traditional Armenian lamb and beef dishes but with suitable vegetarian alternatives.

Montefiore Windmill

OUTSIDE THE OLD CITY WALLS

*Jerusalem began expanding outside the Old City walls in the second half
of the 19th century as Jewish immigration began to increase significantly,
with European churches vying for a presence in the Holy Land.*

> **DISTANCE:** 6km (3.75 miles)
> **TIME:** A full day
> **START:** Montefiore Windmill
> **END:** Ha'Nevi'im Street
> **POINTS TO NOTE:** Dress modestly
> as many of the sites on this tour are
> sacred.

Until the 19th century the Old City walls served as the city limits for Jerusalem residents. Outside was considered dangerous and inhabited by bandits, with the gates closed at nightfall. But overcrowding, squalor, and unsanitary conditions forced residents outside of the walls by the second half of the 19th century.

MONTEFIORE WINDMILL

Opposite the Old City, between the Jaffa Gate and Mount Zion, is the oldest Jewish neighborhood in Jerusalem, **Yemin Moshe**. At the heart of it is the **Montefiore Windmill ❶**, a conspicuous landmark built by the British philanthropist

Sir Moses Montefiore around 1860. It now houses a modest museum (Sun–Thu 9am–4pm, Fri 9am–1pm; free) and a replica of the horse-drawn carriage that Montefiore used to travel across Europe to the Holy Land. The windmill was built to provide flour for **Mishkenot Sh'ananim** (Dwellings of Tranquillity), the long, block-like structure on the steps beneath the windmill, which was also built in 1860 by Montefiore at the bequest of Judah Touro, a Jewish-American philanthropist and businessman.

During the next four years, Montefiore bought an adjoining plot of land and expanded the quarter, calling it Yemin Moshe. There is another windmill behind the Jerusalem Great Synagogue, but the Montefiore Windmill is more well-known. In 1948, it served as an important Israeli observation post during the War of Independence. Following the 1967 Six-Day War, Yemin Moshe was revitalized as an artists' colony. Today its serene walkways and stone houses command some of the highest real estate prices of any neighborhood in the city.

Yemin Moshe

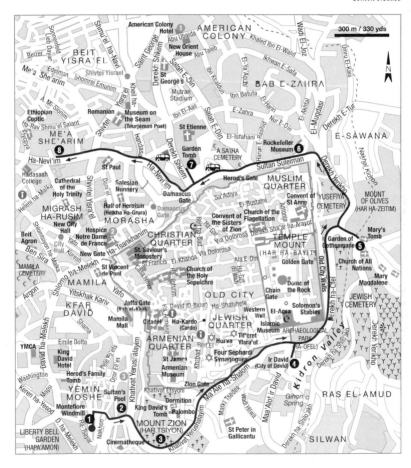

Down the steps from Yemin Moshe is the **Sultan's Pool** ❷. This former reservoir has been converted into an amphitheatre. Located beneath the walls of the Old City, it is one of the world's most inspiring venues for outdoor concerts. At the northern end of Sultan's Pool is **Khutsot ha-Yoster** (Arts & Crafts Lane),

which houses the studios and shops of artists and artisans. Walk through the lane and then up to the Jaffa Gate and along the gardens outside of the Old City to **Mount Zion** ❸. If you're feeling peckish, beneath the Jaffa Gate is **Eucalyptus** ❶, offering a modern take on old classics, in a great location by the city walls.

MOUNT ZION

Legend has it that Suleiman the Magnificent, the Ottoman ruler who completed construction of the Old City walls in 1541, executed his chief architect for forgetting to include **Mount Zion** inside the walls. In Jewish tradition, Zion was an alternative name for Jerusalem; in modern times, Zionism became the secular political Jewish movement for a return from exile in the Diaspora to the Holy Land.

Mount Zion is the site of **King David's Tomb** ❹ (Sun–Thu 8am–5pm, Fri 8am–1pm; free), although some archeologists doubt its authenticity. Above the tomb is the **Coenaculum** (daily 8am–5pm; free), believed to be the Room of the Last Supper. Next to David's Tomb is the **Dormition Abbey** (tel: 02-565 5330; Mon–Sat 8am–5pm; Sun 12.30pm–5.30pm; free), a handsome Benedictine edifice commemorating the place where Mary fell into eternal sleep. The church has a noteworthy mosaic floor and crypt, and its basilica is the site for concerts of liturgical and classical music.

On the eastern slope of Mount Zion on Malki Tsedek Road is the **Church of Peter in Gallicantu** (tel: 02-673 1739; Mon–Sat 8am–5pm; free), which is where Jesus was supposedly imprisoned by the high priest Caiaphas. On the western slope is the Old Protestant Cemetery, the resting place of the British subjects who figured in the religious, cultural, archaeological and diplomatic life of 19th- and early 20th-century Jerusalem. Oskar Schindler, the German industrialist and Nazi Party member who saved the lives of over 1,000 Jews during the Holocaust, is buried in the **Mount Zion Roman Catholic Franciscan cemetery**. The cemetery is located nearby, to the north, and is accessed via Jerusalem University College. Schindler and his wife Emile were posthumously named as Righteous Among Nations by the Israeli government in 1993.

City of David
Find your way back to the main road at the top of Mount Zion (Ma'ale HaShalom Street) and follow it east (downhill). When you get to Dung Gate, keep right for the **City of David** ❺ (www.cityofdavid.org.il; Sun–Thu 8am–5pm or 7pm in summer, Fri 8pm–1pm or 3pm summer; free). This is the original settlement of Jerusalem, built about 1,000 BC after King David captured the city and made it his capital. At the

The Old City, as seen from the Mount of Olives at sunrise

foot of the slope is the **Gihon Spring**, which was, at the time, Jerusalem's only water supply. Since the spring was located in a cave on the floor of the valley, Jerusolomites were in danger of being cut off from their water when the city was under attack. However, a stunning engineering project known as **Hezekiah's Tunnel**, which was carried out by King Hezekiah about 300 years later, connects the Gihon Spring to the Silwan Pool inside the city some 530 meters (580 yards) down the valley.

THE MOUNT OF OLIVES

Continue eastward along the perimeter road beneath the Old City walls; soon the Mount of Olives will come into view. It is believed that Jesus made his triumphal entry into Jerusalem from here. This hill, with its breathtaking view of the Old City, is mainly a Jewish cemetery, dating back to biblical times and still in use today. Jews and Christians believe that the Messiah will lead the resurrected from here into Jerusalem via the Old City's bricked up Golden Gate, which faces the mount.

At the foot of the mount is the handsome **Church of All Nations,** (also known as Gethsemane; daily; free), noted for its Byzantine-style mosaic facade. Adjoining is the **Garden of Gethsemane** ❻ where Jesus was betrayed and adjacent is **Mary's Tomb** (daily 6am–5pm; free). Midway down the stairs of the 5th-century chapel are niches said to hold the remains of Mary's parents, Joachim and Anne, together with her husband Joseph.

For those with the energy to climb up the narrow road to the east (such a detour could take up to an hour), perhaps the most notable church on the way is the **Russian Orthodox Church of Mary Magdalene** (Tue and Thu mornings only; free) built in 1886 with its golden onion-domes. At the top of

Old City Hilltop Views

The Old City can be seen in all its splendor from the surrounding hills, including the Mount of Olives, for those with the energy to climb the hill above the Garden of Gethsemane.

Farther afield is **Mount Scopus**, along the ridge to the north of the Mount of Olives, which is also the site of the Hebrew University, inaugurated in 1925. Among the most impressive sites here is the amphitheater, which boasts an awesome view of the rolling Judean Desert too.

Several kilometers south is the **Armon Hanatziv Promenade**, which also offers a breathtaking view of the Old City and Judean Desert. This is also known as the Hill of the Evil Counsel, where Judas Iscariot is said to have received his 30 pieces of silver.

Inscription at the Garden Tomb

the Mount of Olives is the Seven Arches Hotel, and, perhaps more importantly, you'll be rewarded with the classic picture-postcard view of Jerusalem's Old City (see box).

If you don't fancy the walk, continue north from the Church of All Nations, along Derekh Yerikho, keeping the Old City walls on your left. When you reach the corner of the Old City, cross Sultan Suleiman Street to visit the **Rockefeller Archeological Museum 7** (tel: 02-628 2251; Sun, Mon, Wed, Thu 10am–3pm Sat 10am–2pm; closed Tue, Fri, and holiday eves). Under the auspices of the Israel Museum, the museum is housed in a delightful lime-

Ultra-Orthodox Jew in Me'a She'arim

stone building opened in 1938, and houses a collection of archeological digs conducted during the British Mandate period.

GARDEN TOMB

Carry on along the Sultan Suleiman Street, with the Old City on your left, and turn right at the Damascus Gate. Several hundred meters along Derekh Shkem is the **Garden Tomb 8** (Mon–Sat 9am–noon, 2–5.30pm; free). Within a sumptuous garden, this is a dual-chambered cave that Anglicans and Protestants claim could be the tomb of Jesus. The Garden Tomb is located on a hill which, if viewed from the east, suggests the shape of a skull, thus the belief that it was really here that Christ was crucified and buried.

Farther along Nablus Road is the **American Colony Hotel**, with one of its restaurants, **the Courtyard 2**, a great option for a late lunch or early dinner. This is Jerusalem's oldest hotel and a favorite haunt of foreign journalists because of its neutral location between East and West Jerusalem. Alternatively, the hill to the west of the Damascus Gate is dominated by the splendid 19th-century **Notre Dame de France Hospice 3**, which is opposite the New Gate on HaTsanhanim Street, another excellent option for a meal. The grandiose, ornate French architecture suggests that pilgrims here did not

Notre Dame de France Hospice

suffer deprivation. The building now houses a luxury hotel and cordon bleu French restaurant.

Me'a She'arim

Five minutes' walk northwest from the Garden Tomb is **Me'a She'arim** ❾, Jerusalem's most famous ultra-Orthodox Jewish neighborhood. Built in 1875, the neighbourhood has retained much of the flavour of a *shtetl* – a traditional late 19th/early 20th-century Jewish town found in Central or Eastern Europe. The Jews who live here speak Yiddish and dress traditionally: sidecurls, heavy, black garments for the men and shawls for the women. Signs warning that 'immodest' female dress will not be tolerated should be taken seriously, with offenders often being spat at and cursed.

Ha-Nevi'im (The Street of the Prophets), which runs parallel to the south of Me'a She'arim, is famed for its Ottoman architecture and beautiful buildings. On the corner of Ethiopia Street, for example, is Beit Tavor, built in 1889, which has housed the Swedish Theological Seminary since 1951. The western end of Ha-Nevi'im Street brings you into the center of downtown Jerusalem.

Food and Drink

❶ EUCALYPTUS

Felt alley (between 14 Hativat Yerushalayim and Dror Eliel Street), tel: 02-624 4331; www.the-eucalyptus.com; Sun–Thu 5–11pm; $$$

Just above the Sultan's Pool and beneath Jaffa Gate, Eucalyptus offers an unusual choice of local foods, serving a contemporary interpretation of biblical cuisine beneath the walls of the Old City. Kosher.

❷ THE COURTYARD, IN THE AMERICAN COLONY HOTEL

Nablus Road, Jerusalem, tel: 02-627 9777; 10am–10pm; $$.

The Courtyard, as the name suggests, is located in the courtyard of Jerusalem's oldest and landmark hotel. The restaurant section of this book (see page 103) recommends the Arabesque restaurant in this hotel for a cordon bleu Middle Eastern evening meal. By contrast, the Courtyard is open throughout the day offering gourmet breakfasts, lunches and a lighter dinner.

❸ NOTRE DAME

8 Shivtei Yisra'el Street, tel: 02-628 8018; daily 7–11pm; $$$

Notre Dame is located in the magnificent hospice building of the same name, opposite the Old City's New Gate. Owned by the Vatican, this is one of the city's finest restaurants, and offers surprisingly good-value French fare. Arrive before the restaurant opens for a sundowner in the rooftop bar.

Emek Refa'im Street, German Colony

JERUSALEM'S NEW CITY

From the boulevards of the German Colony, developed by the Templars in the late 19th century, through to Jaffa Road and Makhanei Yehuda market, built up under the British Mandate in the 20th century, the term 'new' can be something of a misnomer.

DISTANCE: 5km (3.12 miles)
TIME: Half day
START: German Colony
END: Makhanei Yehuda market
POINTS TO NOTE: As this is a half-day tour, in the warmer months you might want to consider starting in the late afternoon and ending up in the market, the hub of the city's nightlife. Alternatively, the tour can be split into two tours of two hours each: the first section from the German Colony to the Mamilla Mall; the second to Makhanei Yehuda market.

New Jerusalem is a mishmash of building styles constructed in the final decades of the Ottoman Empire and during the British Mandate in the first half of the 20th century. Architectural harmony is enforced by a local edict requiring all buildings to be faced with local stone. New Jerusalem may lack the affluence of Tel Aviv and the history and religious significance of the Old City, yet it has a pleasing dignity, distinct character and unique charm.

GERMAN COLONY

South of the Old City is the **German Colony**, which was founded in 1873 by German Templars and still has a subtly European air. The central street of the German Colony is Emek Refa'im, a fashionable boulevard of stores, restaurants, and cafés, adjacent to the large Arab-style houses of Baq'a. At the intersection of **Emek Refa'im and Pierre Koenig Street** ❶, you can choose to walk along Emek Refa'im itself, or the parallel railroad park, which has been developed along the tracks of the old Ottoman railroad track.

The First Station
Both routes lead to the **First Station** ❷, a 19th-century Ottoman train station that has been converted into an entertainment center of restaurants and cafés. Opposite the First Station is the Scottish **St Andrew's Church** ❸, which has a well-regarded hospice, and a memorial to the Scottish king Robert Bruce, who, on his death in 1329, requested that his heart be taken to Jerusalem, although it never arrived. Next door is

The YMCA on King David Street

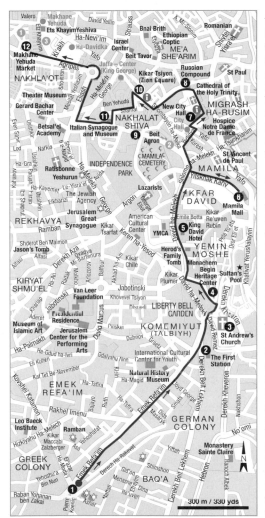

the **Menachem Begin Heritage Center ❹** (tel: 02-565 2020; Sun–Thu 9am–4pm, Fri 9am–noon; free, tours must be reserved in advance). The center includes a museum dedicated to the life of the former prime minister and Nobel Prize winner, Menachem Begin.

King David Street

From the heritage center, walk left on Sh.A. Nakhon Street, and almost immediately take the right fork into David ha-Melekh **(King David Street),** with Liberty Bell Park on your left. **King David Street** hosts two of Jerusalem's most celebrated edifices. The **YMCA,** opened in 1933, has a 36-meter (120ft) tower, offering an outstanding view of Jerusalem, and its symmetrical rotundas reflect an elegant harmony with modern Middle Eastern form. The **King David Hotel ❺**, opposite, was built with old-world grandeur in 1930. It was a British base of command during the Mandate period, and the entire right section of

Mamilla Mall

the building was destroyed in a raid by the Jewish underground in 1946. Visiting heads of state stay in this hotel. Below the King David Hotel, an airy park holds the cavern of **Herod's Family Tomb**, where the stormy monarch buried his wife Mariamne, together with two of his sons after murdering them in a paranoid rage.

Mamilla Mall

At the bottom of King David Street is the **Mamilla Mall** ❻, a 19th-century neighborhood of workshops, now converted into an attractive avenue of fashion outlets, gift stores, and cafés that stretches to the right. Straight on and to the right is Shlomo ha-Melekh Street, which leads to the heart of downtown Jerusalem and Jaffa Road. If you fancy a bite to eat, take a left onto Ben Sira Street, and to **Hummus Ben Sira** ❶. If not, head down Queen Shlomziyon Street (to the right of Ben Sira Street) for around 300 meters/yds until it intersects with Jaffa Road.

JAFFA ROAD

From the late 19th century, Jaffa Road, the main thoroughfare leading from the Old City's Jaffa Gate toward Jaffa, became the main commercial street in New Jerusalem. In the past decade, the road has been reconfigured as a traffic-free precinct, dedicated to the Jerusalem Light Rail, a trolley system that gives the city, and Jaffa Road in particular, a distinctly European flavor.

The new **City Hall** ❼ municipal complex and plaza is just to the right of where Queen Shlomziyon Street joins Jaffa Road. In the basement of City Hall is a model of central Jerusalem used by architects planning new buildings, which can be viewed by the public. City Hall also has a **Visitors' Center** nearby at 3 Safra Square (tel: 02-625 8844; Sun–Thu 9am–4.30pm, Fri 9am–1pm).

Russian Compound

An alleyway to the north of City Hall leads to the **Russian Compound** ❽, which covers several blocks to the right of Jaffa Road. Built in 1864 by Tsar Alexander II to house Russian pilgrims, this complex marked the first notable presence outside the Old City and includes the handsome green-domed **Cathedral of the Holy Trinity** and the Russian Consulate.

DOWNTOWN

On the other side of Jaffa Road are the winding narrow lanes of the recently renovated **Nakhalat Shiv'a** ❾. Founded by Joseph Rivlin in the early 1860s, the enclave had grown to hold some 50 families by the end of that decade.

Rivlin and Salomon Streets house many of the city's favorite restaurants and bars, as well as upscale Judaica stores.

Zion Square

The beating heart of Jaffa Road is **Kikar Tsiyon** (**Zion Square**) ❿, a popular

Tram outisde City Hall

Salomon Street

venue for young Israelis to meet up and for the odd occasional political demonstration. The Jerusalem café scene really gets going near here, along **Ben Yehuda**, the five-block long pedestrian-only avenue that juts out to the west from Zion Square.

From here it is worth the small detour south to Hillel Street to the **Italian Synagogue and Museum** ⑪ (tel: 02-624 1610; www.ijamuseum.org; Sun, Tue, Wed 9am–5pm, Mon 9am–2pm, Thu–Fri 9am–1pm). It was transported here from Conegliano Veneto, near Venice, in 1952 and fully restored by 1989. The original synagogue dates back to 1719.

MAKHANEI YEHUDA MARKET

Continue up Hillel Street to King George Street, the city center's main north-south axis, which will take you back onto Jaffa Road. Some 500 meters/yds up the hill is the **Makhanei Yehuda market** ⑫, which straddles the Jaffa and Agrippas roads. The vendors offer a tempting array of fresh fruitvegetables, spices, and much more, and are usually keen to dispense their political opinions, which, more often than not, lean to the right.

The market is the focus of the city's nightlife with dozens of bars, cafés and restaurants bustling with high energy well into the small hours of the morning. Among the pick of the bars and restaurants are **Crave** ②, serving up delicious US classics, located on neighboring Hashikma Street, and **O'Connells Bar**

②, a lively spot for a drink and a bit of people-watching, in the center of the market.

Food and Drink

① HUMMUS BEN SIRA

3 Ben Sira Street; tel: 02-625 3893; Sun–Thu 11am–11pm Fri 9am–4pm; $

This is a kosher, delicious, and very reasonably priced hummus eatery that has chicken dishes too. Hummus Ben Sira is conveniently located, between downtown and the Mamilla Mall.

② CRAVE GOURMET STREET FOOD

1 Hashikma Street; http://www.facebook.com/gotcrave; Sun–Thu midday–11.30pm, closes Fri afternoon and opens Sat after sunset; $$

Established by an American chef, this cramped eatery serves up US specialties from hamburgers and corned beef sandwiches to tortillas. Kosher.

③ O'CONNELL'S BAR

63 Ets Khayim, Makhanei Yehuda; tel: 02-623 2232; Sun–Thu 1pm–3am, Fri 11am–sunset, Sat after sunset–3am; $

O'Connell's is one of many small bars and eateries in the Makhnei Yehuda market that buzzes with loud music until the early hours of the morning. Just sit down, order a drink and watch the people go by: the high-energy of Jerusalem's night revelers is quite remarkable.

Monastery of the Holy Cross

JERUSALEM'S NATIONAL INSTITUTIONS AND PARKS

Although not universally recognized as Israel's capital, Jerusalem is certainly home to the country's most impressive national institutions such as the Knesset parliament building and Supreme Court, and is surrounded by spacious parks.

DISTANCE: 4km (2.5 miles)
TIME: Half day
START: Monastery of the Cross
END: Jerusalem Railway Station
POINTS TO NOTE: This walk gives you the lie of the land of Jerusalem's parks and national institutions but clearly you cannot go inside and visit all the locations in half a day. You need a full day at least to properly appreciate the exhibits in the Israel Museum.

To the west of the city center, Israel has developed its government precinct and national institutions, separated from the commercial center by a band of attractive hillside parklands. This is the most modern – and carefully planned – part of central Jerusalem, built in the second half of the 20th century.

VALLEY OF THE HOLY CROSS

The most southernmost part of the green strip to the east of the national institutions is the **Valley of the Holy Cross**, which can be reached by taxi, bus route 19, or a half hour walk from the city center. This biblical landscape of olive trees is dominated by the **Monastery of the Holy Cross ❶** (Mon–Sat 9.30am–5pm, Fri 9.30am–1.30pm). Here, it is believed, grew the tree, planted by Abraham's nephew Lot, from which the wood was taken for the cross on which Christ was crucified. The Crusader-style monastery was built in the 7th century and belonged to the Georgian Orthodox Church until the 19th century when it was handed to the Greek Orthodox Church, as the Georgians didn't have the funds to maintain it.

Head southwest from the Valley of the Cross, over Davidzon Square, and you'll find the **Jerusalem Botanical Gardens ❷** (Sat–Thu 9am–5pm, Fri 9am–3pm), home to 6,000 species of international flora, set by a charming lake. **Caffit Restaurant ❶**, just by the lake, opens at 8am and is an excellent spot for a hearty breakfast.

Hebrew University

A road (Derech Brodetski) from the gardens leads up to the **Hebrew Universi-**

The Shrine of the Book at the Israel Museum

ty's **Giv'at Ram Campus**, which includes the science faculties of the university as well as the impressive **Jewish National and University Library ❸** (www.jnul.huji.ac.il; Sun–Thu 9am–7pm, Fri 9am–1pm; free), one of the largest libraries in the world. Among its treasures is the notebook in which Albert Einstein worked out his theory of relativity. This campus was developed between 1948 and 1967, when the original campus on Mount Scopus was cut off by the division of the city. In 2002, a Hamas terrorist detonated a bomb in a busy cafeteria at the Hebrew University, killing nine people and injuring over 100. There is a touching memorial to those killed on the campus.

ISRAEL MUSEUM

From the main exit of the campus at Yig'al Shilo Square, follow Ruppin Street (Derech Ruppin) to the right for the **Israel Museum ❹** (tel: 02-670 8811; www.imj.org.il; Sat–Mon, Wed–Thu 10am–5pm, Tue 4–9pm, Fri 10am–2pm), a leading showcase for the country's art, archeology, and Jewish culture. Opened in

Model of the Second Temple at the Israel Museum

1965, the museum was designed as a hilltop Middle Eastern village, with pavilions like large houses. This has enabled new pavilions to be added over the years as the museum has expanded. There's also a good choice of cafés and restaurants for lunch in the museum, including the **Modern ❷**.

The museum is home to more than 500,000 objects. Its most famous exhibit is the Shrine of the Book, which displays the Dead Sea Scrolls. These scraps of tattered parchment are the oldest known copy of the Old Testament. There is also a Model of the Second Temple in the Israel Museum compound. This impressive 1:50 scale model of Jerusalem in AD 66 conveys just how vast the Second Temple complex was. The price of admission to the museum includes a free shuttle and entry to the **Rockefeller Museum** (see page 40). There is a special wing for children: the Ruth Youth Wing for Art Education with free art classes for children.

Opposite the Israel Museum are two more museums. The **Bible Lands Museum** (tel: 02-561 1066; www.blmj. org; Sun–Thu 9.30am–5.30pm, Wed 9.30am–9.30pm, Fri 9.30am–2pm) in Avraham Granot Street displays artifacts dating from biblical times. The museum explores the culture of the peoples mentioned in the Bible, among them the ancient Egyptians, Canaanites, Philistines, Arameans, Hittites, Elamites, Phoenicians, and Persians.

Along to the northwest is the hands-on **Bloomfield Science Museum** (tel: 02-654 4888; www.mada.org.il; Mon–Thu 10am–6pm, Fri 10am–2pm, Sat 10am–4pm), imaginative and popular with children. The museum places an emphasis on science-related topics. One of its highlights is its bubble-making corner, where huge bubbles can be made using chains and sticks.

KNESSET

Retrace your steps to the Israel Museum, and follow Kaplan Street (opposite). Straight ahead, past the Bank of Israel and the Prime Minister's Office, is the nation's Parliament Building, the **Knesset ❺** (tel: 02-675 3420; www.knesset. gov.il; Mon–Wed open during debates, Sun and Thu 8.30am–2.30pm for guided tours, which must be booked in advance by phone or online). This is the symbol of Israel's democratic system. The current building was opened in 1966 and is influenced by the Greek Acropolis, with added Bauhaus elements.

In addition to the 120-member Knesset plenum, be sure you take the tour of the interior, including tapestries designed by Marc Chagall in the Chagall State Hall, which is used for state banquets. The three large tapestries form an exquisite and colorful decoration for the reception hall and were designed to give a concise and poetic expression to the history and destiny of the Jewish people. The hall also has elegant floor and wall mosaics, which were created by leading Italian artists.

In session at the Knesset

The **Wohl Rose Garden**, in front of the Knesset, is best visited during the spring and late fall. Tucked away to the east of the Knesset along Rothschild Road, above the 40-acre Sacher Park is the **Jerusalem Bird Observatory** (tel: 02 6537 374; Sun–Thu 9am–3pm), one of Israel's many birding stations. The center acts as a magnet for many common migrating and wintering birds: wrynecks, collared flycatchers, masked and red-backed shrikes, and thrush nightingales can be seen migrating; while European robins, hawfinches, and bramblings are regular winter visitors. Many resident Israeli birds also make their home here, including the Palestinian sunbird.

Back past the Knesset is the **Supreme Court ❻** (tel: 02-675 9612; tours in English Sun–Thu at noon). Completed in 1992, this impressive edifice uses light, shade, and glass to great effect. The Supreme Court justices comprise the highest court in the land and have the power to interpret Knesset (parliamentary) legislation.

Go past the Cinema City complex, which is opposite the Supreme Court, and cross the road to your left, and you'll see the **International Convention Center** (Binyanei Ha'Uma). Behind it is the **Yitzhak Navon train station ❼**, which opened in 2018, as well as the central bus station. This is the western entrance to Jerusalem, dominated by the impressive **Bridge of Chords**, a harp-like structure designed by the world-famous architect Santiago Calatrava, which carries the Jerusalem Light Railway. Calatrava was no doubt flattered to design a bridge for the entrance to Jerusalem, but his awe-inspiring design looks a little out of place in this shabby neighbourhood, surrounding the bus station.

From here, it's a five-minute walk down Jaffa Street (just follow the Jerusalem Light Railway) to the Mahanei Yehuda market, if you're in the mood for something to eat or drink.

Food and Drink

❶ CAFFIT

1 Yehuda Burla Street, Jerusalem Botanical Gardens; tel: 02-648 0003; Sun–Thu 8am–11pm Fri: 8am–sunset; $$
Good value sandwiches and light meals, including breakfast in a pastoral setting alongside the botanical gardens lake, with a range of dairy and fish options. Kosher.

❷ MODERN

Israel Museum, 11 Ruppin Street; tel: 02-648 0862; Sun, Mon, Wed, Thu 11.30am–5pm, Tue 11.30am–11 pm, Fri 10am–2pm; $$
In the modernist style after which it is named, the museum's Modern offers a creative Jerusalem meat-based cuisine in an attractive location overlooking the Valley of the Cross and the Knesset. Those wanting a lighter (and cheaper) meal can choose from one of several other cafés in the Museum. You can eat in Modern or any one of the museum cafés without purchasing a ticket to the museum.

Entrance to Yad Vashem

MOUNT HERZL TO EIN KEREM

Mount Herzl, the site of the Yad Vashem Holocaust Museum, overlooks Ein Kerem, the birthplace of John the Baptist and an attractive village with narrow lanes and vineyards nestling in the Jerusalem hills.

DISTANCE: 4km (2.5 miles)
TIME: Half day
START: Mount Herzl
END: Hadassah Hospital Ein Kerem
POINTS TO NOTE: This is a half-day stroll around the hillside but grant a full day if you want to take your time looking around the Yad Vashem Holocaust Museum. Parts of this trip can be easily done most of the year by walking, but in the hot, energy-sapping months, it is best to take a bus or a taxi between Mount Herzl and Ein Kerem, and between Ein Kerem and Hadassah Medical Center.

Mount Herzl is located at the western edge of the city, where Orthodox Jews traditionally came to watch the sunset before evening prayers. Named for the 19th-century founder of modern political Zionism, Theodor Herzl, the hill overlooks the village of Ein Kerem, which was incorporated into the Jerusalem Municipality in 1948, but retains a dis-

tinctive rural character despite its proximity to the city.

MOUNT HERZL

Mount Herzl ❶, which can be reached by using the Jerusalem Light Rail, honors the Viennese journalist Theodor Herzl, who founded the Zionist movement between 1897 and 1904. His remains were transported to Jerusalem in 1949, and his simple black granite tomb marks the summit of the mount. Also buried in the cemetery are Vladimir Jabotinsky and the late Prime Minister Yitzhak Rabin, who was assassinated in 1995, along with other Zionist visionaries. On the northern slope of the ridge is the military cemetery, home to the graves of hundreds of Israeli soldiers who died defending the state.

The **Herzl Museum** (www.herzl.org; Sun–Thu 9am–5pm, Fri 9am–1pm) stands guard at the entrance to the mount, which includes a well-produced audio-visual presentation of Herzl's life, work, and vision.

Yad Vashem exhibit

Memorial to the Deportees, Yad Vashem

YAD VASHEM

The **Yad Vashem World Holocaust Remembrance Center** ❷ (tel: 02-644 3520; www.yadvashem.org.il; Sun–Wed 8.30am–5pm, Thu 8.30am–8pm, Fri 8.30am–2pm) is a striking memorial to the 6 million Jews murdered by the Nazis in the Holocaust. The centerpiece of this complex is the **Holocaust History Museum**, which presents the story of the Holocaust from a uniquely Jewish perspective, emphasizing the experiences of the individual victims through original artifacts, survivor testimonies, personal possessions, photographs, and film footage.

Daring in its design, the museum is housed in a 180-meter (540ft) -long linear structure in the form of a spike (shaped like a Toblerone package), which cuts through the mountain with its uppermost edge – a skylight – protruding through the mountain ridge. Galleries portraying the complexity of the Jewish situation during those terrible years branch off this spike-like shaft. While the exit emerges dramatically, out of the mountainside, affording a view of the valley below. Unique settings, spaces with varying heights, and different degrees of light accentuate focal points of the unfolding narrative.

At the end of the museum's historical narrative is the Hall of Names (a repository for the Pages of Testimony of millions of Holocaust victims), a striking memorial to those who were murdered. From the Hall of Names, continue on to the epilogue and from there to the balcony, with a panoramic view of Jerusalem.

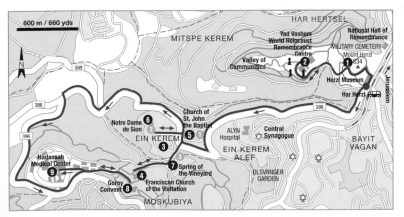

Ein Kerem

The Yad Vashem complex also includes a central chamber, **Ohel Yizkor**, or the **Hall of Remembrance**, which sits on a base of rounded boulders. Inside, an eternal flame flickers amid blocks of black basalt rock engraved with the names of 21 concentration camps. Also well worth visiting is the **Museum of Holocaust Art,** inaugurated in 2005, and located in Yad Vashem's Square of Hope. The museum's rotating permanent exhibition displays some 120 works of art. Most of these works were created during the Holocaust itself, or before the war by artists later murdered in the Holocaust. In total, you will probably need between one and three hours in the complex.

Gorny Convent

EIN KEREM

From Yad Vashem, it is less than 3km (1.6 miles) along Road 386 to **Ein Kerem** ❸ (meaning the spring of the vineyard), a small picturesque biblical village that nestles tranquilly in a valley to the west of Jerusalem. The village is as timeless as the hills and well worth at least several hours visit. The route is clearly signposted and easy to follow; if you don't fancy the walk, take a taxi or bus number 28 from Mount Herzl. There are plenty of restaurants, cafés, and bars in the village for food and drink stops.

In addition to its picturesque cobblestone alleyways and rustic lanes, the history-rich Ein Kerem is compact, with each of its sites a within a few minutes' walk from each other. A Jewish settlement during the Second Temple Period, the village is believed to be the birthplace of John the Baptist. The most renowned sites in the village include the **Franciscan Church of the Visitation** ❹, designed in 1956 by the architect Antonio Barluzzi, on the spot where the Virgin Mary visited Elizabeth, John the Baptist's mother. Nearby is the **Church of St John the Baptist** ❺, also designed by Barluzzi. The mosaics and grotto inside mark the site of the home where it is believed that John the Baptist was born.

At the western edge of the village, on HaOren Street, is **Notre Dame de Sion** ❻, established in 1861 to promote inclusivity between Jews, Muslims, and Christians. The convent has an excel-

Stained-glass windows in the Hadassah Synagogue, designed by Marc Chagall

lent guesthouse; visitors are welcome to come and enjoy the tranquillity of the monastery and its Provence-style vineyards and gardens. It also is home to a **restaurant** ❶ that is an excellent choice for lunch or dinner, although you must make a reservation.

To the south of the village square is the **Spring of the Vineyard** ❼ (also known as the Fountain of the Virgin and St Mary's Spring), which gave the town its name. According to a Christian tradition from the 14th century, the Virgin Mary drank water from this village spring, which is also the place where she and Elizabeth supposedly met. Therefore, since the 14th century, the spring is known as the Fountain of the Virgin. The spring waters are considered holy by some Catholic and Orthodox Christian pilgrims who visit the site and fill their bottles. Above the spring is a disused mosque and minaret. Slightly north of the fountain, back toward the square, is **Pundak Ein Kerem** ❷, serving a good range of hearty Italian dishes.

Farther south, on the hill overlooking the village, is the Russian Orthodox **Gorny Convent** ❽ (Mon–Sat 10am–1pm and 3.30–6pm) with its five distinctive onion-style gold domes. The convent was established in 1871 by the Russian Orthodox Church and the complex contains three churches. Enter the convent from the car park of Hadassah Hospital. It is possible to walk over the hill from Ein Kerem or take a taxi 3km (1.6 miles) around the hill to the hospital.

HADASSAH MEDICAL CENTER - CHAGALL WINDOWS

The **Hadassah Medical Center** ❾, south of the village, is internationally known for Marc Chagall's stained-glass windows in its synagogue, depicting the 12 tribes of Israel (Sun–Thu 8.30am–3.30pm). Distinguished by the richness of their colour, the windows, which were installed in 1962, depict biblical stories.

Food and Drink

❶ **NOTRE DAME DE SION**
23 HaOren Street; tel 02-641 5738; daily 9am–noon and 2–7.30pm; $$
For those looking to eat at a place with Provence-style character and ambience, in a formal white tablecloth French setting, make a reservation at the Notre Dame de Sion.

❷ **PUNDAK EIN KEREM**
9 Ha'Ma'ayan Street; tel: 02-643 1840; daily 9.30am–midnight; $$
The restaurant offers Italian cuisine in a Spanish-style building in the heart of the village, close to the Spring of the Vineyard. The restaurant's fare includes excellent grilled meat and fish dishes, together with an abundance of vegetarian, vegan, and gluten free options.

THE DEAD SEA

At the lowest point on earth, the Dead Sea is surrounded by spectacular desert landscapes. The sea, really an inland lake, contains so much salt that bathers float, while its minerals rejuvenate the skin and have other health benefits.

DISTANCE: 232km (144 miles) round trip (116km/ 72 miles in each direction)
TIME: Full day
START: Jerusalem
END: Ein Bokek and back to Jerusalem
POINTS TO NOTE: While this trip is designed to be undertaken in one day from and back to Jerusalem, there are many hotels by the Dead Sea, which can make this into a two day trip. It is also possible to undertake this day trip from Tel Aviv although the distance is 60km (40 miles) farther.

Located in the Syrian-African Rift Valley, the Dead Sea is 400 meters (1312ft) below sea level. Fed by the River Jordan in the north (most of which has been diverted for irrigation), the Dead Sea is fast evaporating and has already split into two lakes – a larger northern lake and a smaller southern one. Nevertheless, it will likely be many thousands of years before the sea disappears entirely. As well as a salt content of 30 percent,

the Dead Sea contains minerals beneficial to health including bromine, iodine, and magnesium, which act as sedatives to soothe the nerves, easing psoriasis and other skin diseases, rheumatism, arthritis, and respiratory problems. The mud rejuvenates the skin.

The Dead Sea is surrounded by spectacular rocky, barren mountains, which have been a favorite retreat of hermits down the centuries. These include the Essenes, an ascetic sect during the time of Christ to whom the Dead Sea Scrolls belonged. Overlooking the Dead Sea is Masada, a hilltop fortress where Jewish zealots held out against the mighty Roman legion for several years.

DEAD SEA

On arriving from Jerusalem on Highway 1, the first available opportunity to 'float' in the Dead Sea is at **Kalya Beach** ❶ (tel: 02-994 2391; daily 8am–sunset), on the northwest shore near the Lido Junction. Bathing in the Dead Sea is a unique experience: the swimmer bobs around like a cork, and it's possible to read a newspaper

Bathing in the Dead Sea

while sitting on the surface. Non-swimmers can float easily, but must be careful to maintain their balance. The bitter taste of a single drop of Dead Sea water can linger in your mouth all day, while a mouthful should be avoided. Entering the water with major cuts or scratches – or for women who are menstruating – can be extremely painful. It is also possible to drown in the Dead Sea: occasionally the elderly, who are floating on their backs, flip over and do not have strong enough muscles to right themselves. Alternatively, nearby is the Biankini Beach (tel 02-940 0200, daily 9am–sunset).

KUMRAN

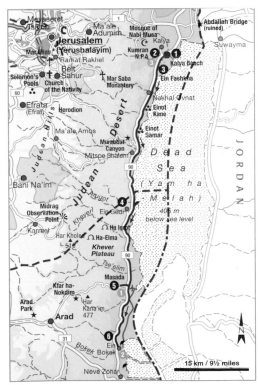

Farther south, on the northwest shore of the Dead Sea is the Essene settlement of **Kumran** ❷ (tel: 02-994 2235; daily 8am–4pm, Apr–Sept until 5pm), where the Dead Sea Scrolls were found. The Essenes, an ascetic Jewish sect of the Second Temple period, deliberately built their community in this inaccessible spot. It was destroyed by the Romans in AD 68. In 1947 a Bedouin shepherd stumbled across the most exciting archeological discovery of the century: scrolls, dating from the time of Christ, preserved in earthenware jars. The scrolls are the oldest known existing copy of the Old Testament.

Searches of the caves unearthed other scrolls and thousands of frag-

The oasis of Ein Gedi

ments, most of which are now on display in Jerusalem, either in the Shrine of the

Bethlehem and Jericho

Bethlehem and Jericho are both in the Palestinian Territories, not far from Jerusalem. To enter the Palestinian Territories you will need to show a valid passport and change taxi or bus. Israeli rental cars cannot be taken in.

Bethlehem, the city of Christ's birth is just 10km (6 miles) south of Jerusalem. In Manger Square is the **Church of the Nativity** (daily dawn–dusk); the original basilica was built in AD 325 by Emperor Constantine the Great and the foundation for it is the crypt revered in Christian tradition as the place where Jesus was born. Beyond the vestibule is the nave; much of this interior dates from Emperor Justinian's rebuilding in the 6th century. Downstairs, is the **Grotto of the Nativity**, where inscribed in Latin is 'Here Jesus Christ was born of the Virgin Mary'. Next door is the **Chapel of the Manger**, where Mary placed the newborn child. Adjoining is the Catholic **St Catherine's**, from which Bethlehem's Midnight Mass on Christmas Eve is broadcast worldwide.

Jericho is 26km (16 miles) east of Jerusalem, just north of the Dead Sea. Highlights of this biblical oasis include the **Monastery of the Temptation**, reached by cable car, and nearby 10,000 year-old archeological remains.

Book at the Israel Museum or in the Rockefeller Archeological Museum. They have revolutionized scholarship of the Second Temple period and thrown new light on the origins of Christianity, indicating that Jesus may have been an Essene, or at least was strongly influenced by the sect.

The partly reconstructed buildings of Kumran are on a plateau some 100 meters (330ft) above the shore and are well worth a visit. Numerous caves, including those where the scrolls were found, are visible in the nearby cliffs, but are not accessible. Near the caves is a tourist center, run by the neighbouring **Kibbutz Kalya**, which also offers accommodation and runs the nearby Kalya Beach. There is a large **restaurant ❶** at Kumran for a late breakfast or early lunch, or refreshing drink.

Ein Fashka

The oasis of **Ein Fashkha ❸** (daily 8am–4pm, Mar–Sept, until 5pm), which is where the Essenes grew their food, is 3km (2 miles) to the south. Today it is a popular bathing site, although only in the fresh water pools. The Dead Sea's alarming evaporation means that there is no longer access to the sea itself here, as it is surrounded by mud and quicksand.

EIN GEDI

Farther south is the lush oasis of **Ein Gedi ❹**, site of a kibbutz, a nature reserve, and another field school, a particularly beautiful spot, with the green-

View over Masada

ery creeping up the steep cliffs beside the springs. **Ein Gedi Nature Reserve** (tel: 08-658 4285; daily 8am–4pm, until 5pm Apr–Sept), founded in 1972, is the home of a large variety of birds and animals, including gazelles, Ibexes, foxes, jackals, and even a few leopards.

The most popular site for hiking and bathing is **David's Spring**, which leads up to a beautiful waterfall, fringed in ferns, where tradition says King David hid from King Saul, when he was on the wrong side of one of the king's rages. According to the biblical account, David crept up on Saul as he slept and cut off a piece of the king's robe, proving he could have killed him but desisted. A tearful reconciliation followed.

On most days during summer and winter, the area around David's Spring is thronged with visitors, so the more energetic may prefer to hike along the course of **Nakhal Arugot**, 1km (0.5 mile) south. This canyon is full of wildlife and has deep pools for bathing. Both Nakhal David and Nakhal Arugot are nature reserves.

Kibbutz Ein Gedi runs a guesthouse, a youth hostel and a spa for bathing in the Dead Sea water and the nearby sulphur springs and mud baths. A camping site, and an additional youth hostel and restaurant are situated on the shore below the kibbutz near the Ein Gedi spa. The nearby beach, once one of the most popular on the Dead Sea, has been closed due to sinkholes, a growing phenomenon associated with the evaporation of the sea.

MASADA

About 20km (12 miles) south of Ein Gedi, towering almost 300 meters (1,000ft) above the Dead Sea shore, is the rock of **Masada** 5 (tel: 08 658 4207; daily 8am–4pm, until 5pm Apr–Sept), one of Israel's most spectacular archeological sites. Part of the line of cliffs that rises up to the Judean desert plateau, Masada is cut off from the surrounding area by steep *wadis* to the north, south and west.

It was on this desolate mesa, in 43 BC, that Herod the Great seized an existing fortress and used it as a retreat from his potentially rebellious subjects. You can wander through the magnificent three-tiered palace that extends down the northern cliff; the Roman bathhouse, with its ingenious heating system; the vast storehouses; the western palace with its fine mosaics; and the huge water cisterns hewn in the rock. You can also appreciate the view of the remarkable desert landscape from the summit, which can be climbed easily from the west via the Roman ramp, ascended by cable car from the east or, more energetically, climbed via the **Snake Path**, also from the east.

These features alone make the fortress worth a visit, but what has made Masada a place of pilgrimage is the story of the epic siege of the fortress: in AD 66 a group of Jewish rebels known as Zealots, and also called the Sicarii – named after the *sica* (dagger), their favorite weapon – seized Masada from

Lathering up in Dead Sea mud

its Roman garrison, an event that triggered the First Jewish–Roman War.

Excavations have uncovered the magnificence of Herod's fortress and palaces, but the most moving finds were of the Zealots' living quarters in the casement wall, their synagogue and ritual baths, the remains of a fire, and fragments of their final meal. The skeletons of a man, woman and child were uncovered in the northern palace; more were found in a nearby cave, where they had apparently been thrown by the Romans.

If you're hungry, the **Masada Food Court** ② is located at the Cable Car Station, and serves fresh juices and light bites to eat.

Food and Drink

① KUMRAN RESTAURANT
Kumran; tel: 02-993 6332; daily 8.30am–5pm; $
A big cafeteria-style restaurant with a self-service buffet designed for large tour groups offers a convenient place for refreshments at good-value prices.

② MASADA FOOD COURT
Masada Cable Car Station; tel: 072-394 5852; daily 11am–4pm; $
Choose the different sections according to the time of day with choices including late breakfasts with fresh juices, as well as heavier – but very reasonably priced – grilled meat meals, hummus, and salads.

③ TAJ MAHAL
Leonardo Inn, Ein Bokek; tel: 050-999 0929; daily midday–midnight; $$
Something of an inappropriate name for a restaurant offering Middle East style fare in an air-conditioned Bedouin tent. Best dishes include hummus, shakshuka, and a range of grilled meats. Kosher.

EIN BOKEK BEACH RESORT

Ensconced along the shore just north of biblical Sodom, is the resort of **Ein Bokek** ❻, featuring several dozen hotels that attract health-seekers from across the globe, with a wide range of accommodation located around the mineral springs. Famous since the 1st century AD, the healing waters are believed to cure a spectrum of ailments, from skin disease to lumbago, arthritis, and rheumatism. The clinics, run by medical staff, offer sulphur baths, mineral baths, salt baths, mud baths, massage, and exercise programs. Smearing yourself with Dead Sea mud may make you look a little ridiculous, but throughout history the mud has been a sought after and effective moisturizer, and was allegedly used on a regular basis by Cleopatra herself, who imported the mud.

There are few exceptional places to eat by the desolate Dead Sea, with Ein Bokek offering the best options, including the misleadingly named **Taj Mahal** ③, which serves a good range of Middle Eastern dishes inside an air-conditioned Bedouin tent.

Tel Aviv beaches

TEL AVIV SEAFRONT – PORT TO PORT

Tel Aviv has 14km (8.7 miles) of golden Mediterranean beaches, all linked by a promenade and cycle path. There is a wide choice of beaches, including gay beaches, a sexually segregated religious beach, and several for dogs.

DISTANCE: 6km (3.75 miles)
TIME: Full day
START: Tel Aviv Port
END: Jaffa Port
POINTS TO NOTE: This trip is designed as a one-day outing, including strolling along the promenade, stops for meals, bathing, and swimming. Children will probably prefer less of the former, and more of the latter two activities. The Mediterranean is deceptively calm with a very strong undertow – drownings are not infrequent so be careful and only swim on the beaches when lifeguards are in attendance. Watch out for jellyfish in June and July.

Tel Aviv has a reputation for being 'cool' and undoubtedly the coolest place in the city – both figuratively and literally – is the beachfront, with the sea breezes tempering the heat and humidity. The central section of the city between ancient Jaffa Port and Tel Aviv port is home to Tel Aviv's most popular beaches, which are often packed during weekends and holidays. If you prefer quieter beaches, visit during the early hours, or in midweek. If you've rented a car, you may wish to head farther north or south, in search of a quieter spot.

The seafront promenade and cafés also throng with leisure seekers, both day and night – this is one of the best places to really feel the slogan that Tel Aviv is 'the city that never stops.' It is also a wonderful spot for people-watching. Both pedestrian paths and cycle tracks line the promenade, the latter being popular with bicycles, electric bicycles, and scooters, which can be rented from the municipal Tel-O-Fun company, or international companies like Mobike, Bird, and Lime.

TEL AVIV PORT

Take a taxi or bus to **Tel Aviv port ❶** to begin your journey. The port actually closed as a working port in 1965 and reopened over a decade ago as an entertainment center with fash-

Opera Tower

800 m / 880 yds

Pedestrian Bridge

TEL AVIV PORT

LITTLE OLD TEL AVIV

Metsitsim Beach

INDEPENDENCE GARDENS

Hilton Beach

Hilton Hotel

Arlozorov

Ben Gurion House

Tel Aviv Marina

Kikar Namir (Atarim)

Gordon Beach

Frischmann Beach

MEDITERRANEAN SEA

Camari Theater

Bograshov

Trumpeldor Beach

Opera Tower

Kikar Bet Be November

Jerusalem Beach

Ge'ula Beach

KEREM HATEIMANIM

Hassan Beq Mosque

Dolphinarium (disused)

CHARLES CLORE PARK

NEVE TSEDEK

Etzel Museum

Beit Ha-Osef Museum

Old Train Station

Noga Theater

Andromeda's Rock ★

Kikar ha-Sokhnut

Clock Tower

Yaffa Port

Museum of Antiquities

Flea Market

She'erit Yisra'el

YAFO OLD CITY

Derekh Ben Tsvi

ionable stores, restaurants, bars, and clubs. There are plenty of cafés here for breakfast before venturing south – try **Café Nimrod** ❶ by the Hangar nightclub. Immediately to the north of the port is the Yarkon River estuary, with a pedestrian bridge crossing toward the chimneys of the Reading power station and the quieter Tel Baruch beaches.

But this walk takes us south to central Tel Aviv. The first beach south of the port is the Metzitzim Beach (meaning Peeper's Beach), named for a 1972 Israeli movie, *Hof Metzitzim*, about teenage boys who peeped through to the showers of the sexually segregated religious beach. This religious beach is also preferred by women who don't want to be harassed. But be sure to come on the right day though: the religious beach is open to women on Sundays, Tuesdays and Thursdays and to men on Mondays, Wednesdays and Fridays. Saturday is mixed day.

Continuing south, the promenade path, for the only section in central Tel Aviv, moves beneath cliffs. A little farther down the path is the first of Tel Aviv's two beaches on which dogs are allowed, located beneath the Hilton hotel and Independence Park. This beach is followed by the Tel Aviv's main gay beach. In between these two beaches is the Hilton Beach itself, which is considered the best in the city for surfing.

Volleyball on the beach

Gordon Beach and Tel Aviv Marina

TEL AVIV MARINA

Continuing south is **Tel Aviv Marina** ❷, and the adjacent Gordon (salt water) swimming pool. The marina rents out boats, and surfboards and equipment for water sports. Qualified divers can also rent diving equipment here; diving lessons are available too. The marina is overlooked by Kikar Atarim, which is slated for redevelopment. The coastline here is dominated by an imposing row of hotels overlooking the city's busiest beaches – Gordon, Frishman, and Bograshov – before the **Opera Tower** ❸ at the junction of Allenby Street and Retsif Herbert Samuel Street. Each hotel has its own beach strip with showers, easy chairs, and refreshment amenities that are all open to the public.

The beach bar and restaurant at **La Mer** ❼, by Bograshov Beach, is a great place with to relax over a meal or enjoy a drink.

Beach Sports

Beach volleyball is becoming increasingly popular in Tel Aviv, and a number of courts have been set up near Gordon Beach. However by far the most popular beach sport is *matkot*, a uniquely Israeli activity in which a small ball is batted backwards and forwards between participants, with no winners and losers. It's a bit like frisbee, except it is played a bat and ball and accompanied by an incessant clacking sound. Perhaps the most popular *matkot* spot is Geula Beach (also known as Jerusalem Beach), just to the south of Opera Tower.

Marking the end of the hotel line to the south near the **Hassan Beq mosque** ❹ are the David Intercontinental and Dan Panorama hotels. During the 1980s the mosque, which dates back to Ottoman times, had become dilapidated and was sold to an entrepreneur so that he could convert it into a nightclub. This decision sparked furore throughout the Muslim world; consequently, a political arrangement was reached whereby the Egyptian government bought and restored the mosque. Today, they are still responsible for its upkeep.

Just to the south, on the edge of the Neve Tzedek neighborhood is the **Old Train Station** ❺, now a complex of stores and restaurants, once a 19th-century Ottoman train station at the end of the Jerusalem–Jaffa line. Farther south just by the seafront is Charles Clore Park, a 12-hectare (30-acre) area of greenery overlooking the sea that is popular barbecue spot on Saturdays and holidays.

Within the park is the **Etzel Museum** ❻ (2 Nahum Goldman St; Sun–Thu 8.30am–4.30pm; tel: 03-517 7180) with a striking exterior design combining stone and glass. Inside the museum documents the story of the pre-state right-wing paramilitary underground organization. The museum is

Jaffa

near the Alma Beach, which also has a dog section, located just north of Jaffa. The Maaravi (Western) Beach, just before you enter Jaffa, is also popular with surfers.

JAFFA

Enter Jaffa along what is called the Sea Barriers Promenade. Here there is no beach, just sea wall. In the winter months, when there are high winds you may catch a bit of sea spray. The promenade enters **Jaffa's ancient port ❼**, which still houses local fishermen. It was from here that Jonah set sail on his ill-fated voyage and King Solomon imported cedar wood from Lebanon to build the Sec-

ond Temple. Offshore is a cluster of rocks, the largest of which, according to local legend, was the very rock to which Andromeda was chained in Greek mythology.

End the day at one of the charming dockside restaurants, which reputedly serve up the fresh catches of the local fishermen. **The Old Man and the Sea ❸** is a Jaffa institution and one of best restaurants along the dockside.

Although our walk ends here, the Promenade and beaches continue farther south through Jaffa, and onto Bat Yam and Rishon Lezion, with many more kilometers of golden sands and the blue Mediterranean to explore.

Food and Drink

❶ CAFÉ NIMROD

8 Hangar, Tel Aviv port; tel: 077-213 3007; daily 9am–1am; $

Set yourself up with a classic, hearty, and healthy Israeli breakfast with a selection of salads, vegan options, eggs and more, all served up with a delightful view of the Mediterranean.

❷ LA MER

91 Herbert Samuel Street, Tel Aviv; tel: 03-523 7822; open daily 7am–3am; $$

La Mer beach bar and restaurant is quite

literally on Bograshov Beach, and serves a delicious range of breakfasts, lunches, and dinners. It's also a great place to stop for a refreshing drink and a bit of people watching.

❸ THE OLD MAN AND THE SEA

101 Retzif Ha'alyah Hashnia, Jaffa; tel: (03) 544 8820; open daily 11am–midnight; $$

Middle-Eastern restaurant serving an excellent mezze salad spread, and tasty grilled meats and fish. The waiters put on an impressive show collecting up all the plates in one go, however large the number of diners.

JAFFA

The narrow alleyways and fishing port of ancient Jaffa, sometimes described as the world's oldest harbor, contrast delightfully with the modernity of Tel Aviv, its brash neighbor immediately to the north.

DISTANCE: 2km (1.25 miles)
TIME: Half day
START: Clock Tower
END: Clock Tower
POINTS TO NOTE: This is a hilly walk, and not recommended for young children. This circular walk around Jaffa does not include the Old Port, which is featured in the seafront walk (route 7) and the flea market, featured in the markets tour (route 10).

Old Jaffa (also spelled Yafo) became part of the Tel Aviv-Jaffa Municipality in 1951 but is several millennia older than the adjoining city to the north. The port was captured by the Egyptians 3,500 years ago and there are archeological finds here from 20,000 years ago. Subsequently, Alexander the Great, Herod, Richard the Lionheart, Napoleon, and the Ottoman Turks (among others), have all passed through Jaffa, alternately destroying and building, before the British arrived in 1947 and the Israelis took over in 1948.

Although Jaffa is mentioned on several occasions in the Bible as the port closest to Jerusalem, there are no sacred Jewish sites here. Christians, however, revere Simon the Tanner's house as the place where Christ's disciple Peter is said to have received divine instruction to preach to the gentiles (non-Jews).

Extensive restoration and high-end construction in recent decades have transformed Jaffa into a labyrinth of art galleries, upscale stores, expensive apartments, and hotels. However, the area still retains its ancient charm.

CLOCK TOWER

Old Jaffa begins at the **Clock Tower** ❶ on Yefet Street, which was built in 1906 by the Turks. The clock tower's stained-glass windows each portray a different chapter in Jaffa's long and colorful history. To the east of the clock tower at 7 Yefet Street is **Abouelafia** ❶, one of Tel Aviv's best-loved bakeries and a great place to grab a snack. . Having opened in 1879, Abouelafia is as much a local landmark as the clock tower itself.

Minaret of the Jama El-Baher Mosque

Facing what used to be local police station is the **Setai**, a luxury hotel that opened in 2018. The original building was erected by the Ottomans in the 19th century in the style of a fortress, which served as the home and the administrative buildings of the Saray (the Turkish ruler of Jaffa). In recent decades it served as the local police station and prison, before being converted into a hotel.

Mahmoudiya Mosque

From the clock tower, walk past the Setai westward along Mifrats Shlomo Street. On the left is a parade of fish restaurants, while on your right, an entrance leads to the **Mahmoudiya Mosque ❷**, the largest mosque in Jaffa. Construction of the mosque began in 1730 and was completed in 1812, when it was named after Jaffa's then-governor, Muhammad Abu Nabbut. Inside the complex are two large courtyards and a smaller inner courtyard, while the mosque itself has arcades and a large rectangular prayer hall, covered by two big shallow domes, and topped by the slender, elegant minaret.

Museum of Antiquities

A few hundred meters/yds along the road is the **Jaffa Museum of Antiquities ❸** (Sun–Thu 9am–1pm, also Tue 4–7pm, Sat 10am–2pm), where archeological exhibits from many years of excavations trace the city's development. The building itself was constructed in the 18th-century by the Turks; later it won acclaim throughout the Middle East as the soap factory of the Greek Orthodox Damiani family. The sidewalk opposite the museum overlooks the sea, and it is worth stopping to take in the splendid view of the coastline, beaches, and Tel Aviv to the north.

KEDUMIM

Up the hill to the south is the Franciscan **St Peter's Church,** located on one side of **Kikar Kedumim ❹**, the main square of Old Jaffa. The **St Louis Monastery** in the courtyard was named

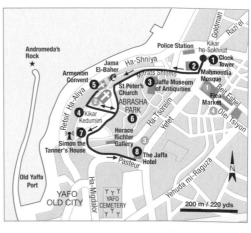

Alley in Jaffa

The Gate of Faith, Abrasha Park

after the French king, who stayed here in 1147 during the Second Crusade. The monastery later served as a hostel for pilgrims to Jerusalem and was known in the 17th century as the "Europeans' House". Napoleon also stayed here after conquering Jaffa. If you are hungry, try **Abrage** ❷ for an excellent fish dish.

A little way to the west toward the sea is the minaret of the **Jama El-Baher Mosque,** located next door to the first 'modern' Jewish house in Jaffa, which was built in 1820. The **Armenian Convent** ❺ and church here mark the site of a 17th-century pilgrims' inn. A magnificent renovated Turkish mansion behind the museum, once a Turkish bath house, has been converted into a nightclub and restaurant, El-Hamam.

Abrasha Park ❻, above Kikar Kedumim, is home to an amphitheater that often has free music concerts during summer. One of the hills has a fascinating sculpture depicting biblical tales such as the fall of Jericho, the sacrifice of Isaac, and Jabor's dream of a ladder ascending to heaven. The peak of the hill in Abrasha Park offers the finest view of Tel Aviv, from the seafront to the gleaming high-rise, high-tech towers. From here, **Horoscope Path** begins to wind its way through the Jaffa wall and then goes all the way to the lighthouse at the wall's southern entrance, on the corner of Shimon Haburski.

SIMON THE TANNER'S HOUSE

Head back down to **Kikar Kedumin**. It's well worth taking a look at the excavations here, which give a glimpse into the city's multi-faceted history. This is also one of Tel Aviv's most popular evening spots.

Down an alleyway to the right is **Simon the Tanner's House** ❼ (daily 8am–7pm) where, in addition to performing miracles such as raising Tabitha from the dead, Peter is believed to have received divine instruction to preach to non-Jews (act 9: 36–42).

On the southern side of the wall, along Pasteur Street, a modern structure rather spoils the beauty of the

Entrance to Simon the Tanner's House

Jaffa's Clock Tower

ancient walls. This is a shopping area, which has a number of restaurants and cafés. Farther along Pasteur Street is the **Horace Richter Gallery**, which displays the work of local artists.

The Jaffa

Back down at the corner of Pasteur Street and Yefet Street is yet another opened luxury hotel, the **Jaffa 8**. A 19th-century hospital and monastery has been transformed into a state-of-the-art 21st- century luxury hotel, with the arched colonnades and stained-glass windows retained in a remarkable renovation project. If you're feeling affluent, pamper yourself with an expensive meal in the hotel's excellent restaurant, **Don Camillo 3**.

Turn left back down Yefet Street and you will come full circle by returning to the Clock Tower and the Abouelafia bakery, if you fancy a snack. Alternatively, for a little more sustenance, the streets inland around the nearby flea market are filled with great restaurants and eateries, including **Hummus Danny 4**.

Food and Drink

1 ABOUELAFIA BAKERY

7 Yefet Street; tel: 03-681 2340; always open; $
For 140 years Jaffa's landmark Arab bakery has been feeding residents and visitors alike with a range of mouthwatering Middle Eastern breads, including its specialty, *sambousak*, with various delicious fillings. The only drawback is that there is nowhere on the premises to eat. This is the bakery that never stops (it is open 24 hours a day, 7 days a week) in the city that never stops.

2 ABRAGE

6 Kedumim Square; tel: 03-524 4445; daily 9am–midnight; $$$
This restaurant, set in the heart of Old Jaffa inside an Ottoman building next to St Peter's church, specializes in fish and seafood, and has a great atmosphere.

3 DON CAMILLO

2 Louis Pasteur Street; tel: 03-778 5660; open daily 7–11pm; $$$$
This opened high-end restaurant is in the luxury Jaffa Hotel in a converted monastery combining 21st-century luxury with 19th-century grandeur. This is an Italian restaurant, with the New York-trained chefs giving the dishes a distinctly American twist. Kosher.

4 HUMMUS DANNY

8 Olei Zion Street, Jaffa; tel: 052-327 6229; Sun–Thu 10am–10pm Fri 9am–4pm; $
Offering great value hummus and other Mediterranean dips, this veteran eatery, located in the heart of Jaffa's flea market, is perfect for a light meal. There are plenty of vegan options too. Kosher.

Rothschild Boulevard

BAUHAUS - CENTRAL TEL AVIV

Tel Aviv is home to several thousand Bauhaus buildings – a distinctive minimalist style developed in Europe during the 1920s and 30s – which is by far the world's largest collection of such buildings.

DISTANCE: 4.5km (2.75 miles)
TIME: Half day
START: Western end of Rothschild Boulevard
END: Yitzhak Rabin Square
POINTS TO NOTE: This walk is also not recommended for children as it involves mainly looking at the city's buildings.

Part of Tel Aviv, known as the White City, was designated a Unesco World Heritage Site in 2003 thanks to its unique collection of gleaming white Bauhaus-style buildings. Beneath Tel Aviv's imposing high-tech glass towers, it can be difficult to pick out the Bauhaus buildings. The understated cubic style is often hidden away behind trees, and in many cases urban grime and decay, which is ironic given the area's name. Thankfully though, the money pouring into the city's high-tech industry has enabled many of the buildings to be restored to their former glory. However, the original Tel Aviv Bauhaus architects, driven by minimalist,

ascetic, and socialist ideals, many of whom were German Jews fleeing Nazi persecution, might not have approved of the restoration, which often includes the addition of a penthouse and other expensive add-ons. Most of Tel Aviv's Bauhaus buildings can be seen along Rothschild Boulevard and the adjoining streets, through to Dizengoff Street to the north.

ROTHSCHILD BOULEVARD

We begin this tour at the western end of **Rothschild Boulevard** ❶, part of the original Tel Aviv garden suburb that was established in 1909. Built over a dried riverbed, the boulevard is Tel Aviv's most elegant address, featuring a central promenade dotted with trees, benches, and refreshment stands, as well as a cycle path. At the western end of the street, which predates the Bauhaus style, buildings are of an eclectic nature, combining European and Ottoman styles.

This is the heart of Tel Aviv's financial district and there are several

Bauhaus architecture on Rothschild Boulevard

museums here too. The **Independence Hall**, at number 16, the former residence of the city's first mayor, Meir Dizengoff. The Declaration of Independence was signed here on 15 May 1948, and it was also the first home of the Knesset (parliament) until it moved to the Opera Tower building on the beach, and then to Jerusalem. The second and third floors comprise the **Bible Museum** (Sun–Fri 9am–1pm, Sat 10am–2pm).

Across the road is the **Israeli Defense Forces Museum** (Ha Haganah; tel: 03-560 8264; Sun–Thu 9am–4pm), located in the former residence of Haganah commander Eliahu Golumb. **Breuer House ②**, at number 46, was built in 1922, and has tiny decorative balconies, a pagoda-like wooden roof, a minaret, and a large, enclosed garden. On the verge of demolition in 1948, it was saved when the Soviet ambassador requested it for his headquarters. It served as the Soviet Embassy until 1953, when diplomatic relations between Israel and the **USSR** were severed. Renovated in the 1990s, it now houses Sotheby's Israel offices.

BAUHAUS BEGINS

Typical Bauhaus-style buildings can be seen farther east along Rothschild Boulevard. Both numbers 61 and 71 have been restored to their original pristine white condition. Numbers 89, 91, and 140 are more examples, and nearby Engel Street to the right, is a delightful mews full of Bauhaus buildings.

Sheinkin Street ❸, one of the city's trendiest thoroughfares, stretches east from Rothschild Boulevard. It is the bastion of Israel's trendy, leftist, and secular

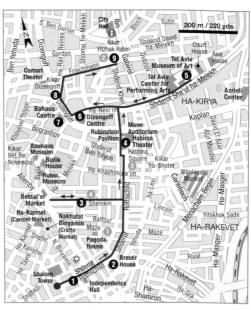

Habima Theater　　　　　　　　　*Monet's paintings at the Museum of Art*

community, although the ultra-Orthodox Lubavitchers (Habad) have their Tel Aviv headquarters in Sheinkin too.

Sheinkin is renowned for its leading fashion designs, and for hip Tel Avivians. **Rubinsky House** at 65 Sheinkin Street is a superb example of a restored Bauhaus building. If you're feeling hungry, the nearby **Orna and Ella** ① is a good option for a quick bite to eat.

HABIMA SQUARE

Head back to Rothschild Boulevard, and follow it north for Tel Aviv's premier cultural complex, a large municipal square that includes the **Habima Theater** ④, the **Mann Auditorium**, and the **Rubinstein Pavilion**. During the Russian Revolution, a group of young Russian-Jewish actors formed a collective and dreamed of a Hebrew theater. The dream came true in Tel Aviv, dozens of years later. The Habima Theater (Habima means 'the stage' in Hebrew), built on the square of the same name, originally had creaking wooden chairs and lousy acoustics: today it has two theaters (one seating 1,000 and a smaller one with seats for 300), revolving stages, and simultaneous translation into several languages during the high season.

On the southern side of the square near the end of Rothschild Boulevard is **Lachmanina** ②, a great place for a meal or just a drink to watch the world go by.

Just next to the theatre is the **Charles Bronfman Auditorium**, the home of the Israel Philharmonic Orchestra. Tickets here are highly prized and hard to get. The third building in this complex is the **Rubinstein Pavilion** (tel: 03-528 7196; Mon, Wed 10am–4pm, Tue, Thu 10am–10pm; Fri 10am–2pm, Sat 10am–4pm), a branch of the Tel Aviv Museum of Art, which specializes in modern art exhibitions.

The main part of the **Tel Aviv Museum of Art** ⑤ (tel: 03-607 7020; www.tamuseum.co.il; Mon, Wed, and Sat 10am–4pm, Tue, Thu 10am–10pm, Fri 10–2pm), is several minutes' walk away: to get there, go north on Shlomo Ibn Gbriol Street for two blocks and right onto Shaul Hamelekh Boulevard. The museum has four central galleries, an auditorium that often features movie retrospectives,

Inside the Tel Aviv Museum of Art

Café on Dizengoff Street

numerous other halls, a sculpture garden, a cafeteria, and a store. There are exhibitions of 17th-century Dutch and Flemish masters, 18th-century Italian paintings, Impressionists, post-Impressionists, and a good selection of 20th-century art from the US and Europe, in addition to modern Israeli work.

Next to the museum is the **Tel Aviv Center for Performing Arts**, which was inaugurated in the 1990s. This attractive new building includes the New Israel Opera as well as both a theater and auditorium.

DIZENGOFF

Retrace your steps back toward Habima Square, but this time turn right on Dizengoff Street from Shlomo Ibn Gbriol. This was once the city's most fashion-

Tel Aviv Center for Performing Arts

able thoroughfare and although less grand today, it is still one of Tel Aviv's principal streets. Café-going is a major part of any self-respecting Tel Avivian's way of life. Some people go to cafés for their first coffee of the day; others conduct business meetings, or entertain guests. On a sunny day you may get the impression that the entire city is on holiday, sipping coffee at sidewalk cafés.

Continue down Dizengoff, passing Habima Square on your left, to the **Dizengoff Center ⑥**, a modern multi-level shopping complex offering everything from offbeat pets to Oriental carpets, complete with movie theaters, restaurants, sports shops, and banks.

Bauhaus Center

Just over a block north from the Dizengoff Center is the **Bauhaus Center ⑦** (77 Dizengoff Street; tel: 03-522 0249; www.bauhaus-center.com; Sun–Thu 10am–7pm Fri 10am–2.30pm Sat 10am–7.30pm), which tells the full story of the city's Bauhaus buildings with displays and changing exhibitions. A weekly tour (in English) of Tel Aviv's Bauhaus buildings leaves from here every Friday at 10am.

Farther north is **Dizengoff Square ⑧**, which is home to some of the finest examples of Bauhaus architecture in the city. One such example is the **Cinema Hotel**. Originally built in the 1930s as a movie theater, the building was recently restored and transformed into a boutique hotel.

Yitzhak Rabin Square

Art Galleries

Continue north on Dizengoff Street for two blocks, until it intersects Gordon Street. Turn left on Gordon and take the second left onto Dov Hoz Street, the heart of Israel's art gallery scene. Works of the great masters, such as Picasso and Chagall, are displayed here beside paintings by leading Israeli artists such as Agam, Gutman and Kadishman. Although these works are displayed in galleries, which are essentially stores, it is the Tel Aviv custom to walk in, around, and out of these stores, as if in a museum.

YITZHAK RABIN SQUARE

Re-join Gordon Street from Dov Hoz and turn right, following the road to the central square of the city, **Yitzhak Rabin Square** ❾. It was here, when it was then known as Kikar Malchei Yisrael, on 4 November 1995, that Prime Minister Yitzhak Rabin was assassinated by a right-wing extremist gunman, immediately after a huge demonstration in support of the peace process. The square was immediately renamed Yitzhak Rabin Square, and there is an unusual black memorial close to the spot where he fell, at the northern end of the square, just behind the steps to the City Hall. Portraits, paintings, and graffiti cover the area as a touching and varied memorial to a man respected by many of differing convictions.

There are many fine restaurants and cafés around Yitzhak Rabin Square, including Vietnamese restaurant **Ca Phe Hanoi** ❸.

Food and Drink

❶ ORNA AND ELLA

33 Sheinkin Street; tel: 03-525 2085; daily 10am–midnight; $$

What started out as a café on trendy Sheinkin Street has now developed into a bistro with an emphasis on homemade breads, pastries, and pastas.

❷ LACHMANINA

4 Marmorek Street; tel: 03-536 2124; Sun–Thu 7am–11pm, Fri 7am–5pm; $

This café, which overlooks Habima Square, specializes in its own freshly baked breads and pastries as well as specialty dishes like shakshuka sandwich and caramel pie.

❸ CA PHE HANOI

3 Malkhei Yisrael Street; tel: 03-677 1184; Sun–Thu noon–midnight, Fri 10am–4pm, Sat 9pm–midnight; $$

Beneath the Tel Aviv Municipality building at Yitzhak Rabin Square, this restaurant offers Vietnamese food, with Middle Eastern and French influences. It is one of the few quality Asian restaurants in Tel Aviv that is kosher.

Clothing stalls at Jaffa's Flea Market

MARKETS OF TEL AVIV

Tel Aviv is as much a city of markets as it is a high-tech hub. From antiques, and arts and crafts, to fresh fruit and vegetables, spices and clothes, don't miss your chance to sample the finest wares Tel Aviv has to offer.

DISTANCE: 5.5km (3.4 miles)
TIME: Half day
START: Jaffa's flea market
END: Sarona Market
POINTS TO NOTE: This may be in the Middle East, but Tel Aviv very much sees itself as a European city, so for the most part prices – especially on smaller purchases – are fixed rather than bargained for, except for possibly some of the more exotic goods in the flea market. This is not a walk for children, unless they happen to love markets. All the city's markets are open Sunday to Thursday and Friday until lunchtime and closed Saturday.

Tel Aviv has always had great markets. In the past two decades, the huge injection of high-tech money has enabled the city's markets to expand: where they were once cheap and shabby, bustling with buyers competing for bargains, the markets are now filled with middle-class Israeli shoppers looking for an alternative to the soulless malls dominated by the large retail chains and mass-produced items. Nevertheless, there are still bargains to be found in markets that are more tourist-friendly and attractive than ever.

JAFFA FLEA MARKET

Begin your market odyssey at **Jaffa's Flea Market** ❶ known locally as Shuk Hapishpishim. The market is located in the narrow streets and alleys of Jaffa, to the southeast of the clock tower, the start and end point of route 8. It specializes in antiques, furniture, woodcrafts, copperware, jewelry, and bric-a-brac, with a major emphasis on Judaica as well as Arab, Persian, and Indian items, including exotic clothing.

Olei Zion Street is the heart of the market. The task of the shopper here is to sort the genuine from the junk, in the stands and the stores. However, as often as not, beauty is in the eye of the beholder and the price is often negotiable. The flea market is also a great place to have breakfast or brunch: try **Café Puaa** ❶ for an excellent Israeli breakfast.

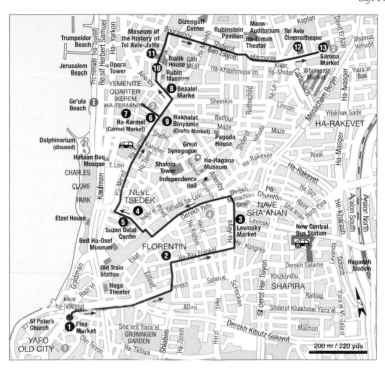

Florentin

To the northeast of the flea market, reached by following Shalma Road (the northern extremity of the market) for just under one kilometre, is the shabby, ramshackle neighbourhood of **Florentin ❷**. Turn left into Nahlat Binyamin Street, which runs the length of Florentin, considered Tel Aviv's trendiest and most bohemian quarter, with a flourishing nightlife, often compared to New York's Meatpacking District or London's Hoxton. The rents here have become so high that many young people are leasing in Givat Shapira, the even shabbier neighborhood to the east, which will probably become the next trendy quarter.

LEVINSKY MARKET

Farther along Nahlat Binyamin, near the intersection with Levinsky Street is the

Shabazi Street in Neve Tzedek

Levinsky Market ❸, one of Tel Aviv's top foodie hotspots. This market sells the most exotic spices in Israel, as well as a diverse range of dried fruits and nuts of Arab, Greek, Persian, and Balkan origin. The market is also the place to go to for coffee connoisseurs, and a range of pastries and *burekas* are for sale in a neighborhood that was originally settled by Persian and Greek Jewish immigrants.

Neve Tzedek

Walk the length of Levinsky Street westward and then across Derech Jaffa into Pines Street to reach **Neve Tzedek ❹**. The neighborhood was founded in 1887 as a suburb of Jaffa, pre-dating Tel Aviv itself. Today it is a picturesque maze of narrow streets flanked by gentrified low-built Arab-style houses. At the time the quarter was considered a luxury suburb, despite the crowded housing and less-than-sanitary conditions. In recent years the quarter's quaint old dwellings have taken the fancy of artists and well-to-do businesspeople, who have restored them, constructed new buildings, and replanted the inner courtyards. One such resident is Russian billionaire and Chelsea Football Club owner Roman Abramovich, who bought the six-bedroom Varsani Boutique hotel in Shabazi Street in 2015 for $27 million, and added a two-story extension.

Suzan Delal Center

Shabazi Street is the main thoroughfare of cafés and fashion stores in Neve Tzedek. At its southwestern end is the **Suzan Dalal Center ❺**, the site of the city's first all-girls' school, incidentally also the first all-Hebrew school in Israel. Today the building is home to the **Batsheva Dance Company** and the **Inbal Dance Company**. With the theater's opening, in a magnificent plaza dotted with orange trees, several colorful galleries, restaurants and nightclubs popped up in the area, lending a new vitality to the century-old streets.

CARMEL MARKET

At the southwestern end of Shabazi Street, turn right into Hevrat Shas Street and then right again into Mered Street. Continue past the two large hotels on your left (Dan Panorama and David Intercontinental) and you will reach the entrance to the **Carmel Market ❻** by the Carmelit bus depot. Open Sundays to Thursdays from early in the morning until 7pm, and until 2pm on Fridays (the market's busiest day), the market stretches along the narrow Hacarmel Street all the way to Allenby Street.

Unlike Makhanei Yehuda market in Jerusalem, which has spread out over the adjoining streets, most of the Carmel Market is on one road. Most of the vendors at the southern end of the market sell fresh produce and other goods, while clothes and electronic goods prevail at the northern end. A large variety of exotic fruits, vegetables, and herbs can be found here, as well as clothes, shoes,

Carmel Market   Glassware for sale on Nakhalat Binyamin

pickled foods, and flat bread, all at bargain prices. Despite appearances to the contrary, the market is very westernized and haggling is not appreciated.

Kerem Hatamanim

The market also has many small cafés and restaurants that remain open at nights and on Saturdays. There are also many eateries in the streets immediately to the west in the **Yemenite Quarter (Kerem Hatamanim)** ❼, which is a great place for lunch. The quarter's exotic winding streets are a jolt back in time, preserving the look and feel of the Yemenite community that settled here more than a century ago. Here, in the restaurants housed in the Arab-style stone buildings, are many of the best places to sample the spicy, pungent Yemenite cuisine, like **Erez Yemenite Restaurant** ❷.

BEZALEL MARKET

At the northern end of Carmel Market, immediately across Allenby Street and along King George Street is the **Bezalel Market** ❽, which is concentrated in Beitlehem Street, the first left off King George Street. In terms of clothes, shoes, bags, underwear, and lingerie, everything is available here at bargain prices, from the best-known brands to exotic treasures. There is also a section for carpets and rugs. As with Carmel Market, Bezalel Market is open Sunday to Thursday from early until 7pm, until 2pm on Friday, and is closed on Saturday.

Nakhalat Binyamin
Back at the junction where Carmel Market meets Allenby Street, opposite King George Street, is a traffic-free street called **Nakhalat Binyamin** ❾. Here, on Tuesdays and Fridays, arts and crafts traders bring their wares to parade and sell. This is a great place for gift-shopping, as the artisans combine jewelry with juggling, cactus plants with camel-leather bags, and wood carvings with wonderful art. On these days, the street-side cafés here are crowded.

Bialik Street
Turn left on Allenby Street. A couple of blocks down on the right is **Bialik Street** ❿, another pleasant street dating from the city's early days. At number 14 is the **Rubin Museum** (tel: 03-525 5961; www.rubin museum. org.il; Mon, Wed–Thu 10am–3pm, Tue 10am–8pm, Sat 11am–2pm), the former residence of Israeli artist Reuven Rubin. A short walk from here is **Bialik House** (tel: 03-525 4350; same hours as Rubin House), once the home of Israel's national poet, Haim Nahman Bialik. Built in 1925, it has a little tower and dome, together with a prominent pink balcony and arched columns, like those of the Doge's Palace in Venice. Nearby is the **Museum of the History of Tel Aviv-Jaffa** ⓫ (27 Bialik Street; tel: 03-724 0311; Mon– Thu 9am–5pm Fri–Sat 10am–2pm), located in what was the old Tel Aviv municipality building.

Sarona Market

Food and Drink

① CAFÉ PUAA

8 Rabbi Yohanan Street; tel: 03-682 3821; Sun–Fri 9am–1am, Sat 10am–1am; $

This veteran establishment, located in the heart of the Jaffa flea market, offers great value Israel-style breakfasts throughout the day as well as quirky tasty dishes like pumpkin dumplings. This is also a great place to hang out and eat and drink at night, when the market comes back to life.

② EREZ YEMENITE RESTAURANT

28 Nakhliel Street, Kerem Hatemanim; tel: 052-255 3808; Sun–Thu 10am–8pm, Fri until 4pm, closed Sat; $

This is a traditional family restaurant in the heart of the city's Yemenite quarter (Kerem Hatemanim). Start off with the classic Yemenite soup and pita; house specialties include meatball and okra in tomato sauce, as well as a range of grilled meat and fish dishes.

③ CAPTAIN CURRY

3 Aluf Kalman Magen Street, Sarona Market; tel: 03-609 5960; Sat–Thu noon–10pm, Fri 11am–4pm; $$

Under the supervision of one of Israel's top chefs, Jonathan Roshfeld, this is one of the best Sarona Market eateries and a great place to grab a quick, filling, and delicious curry. Captain Curry offers large portions at good-value prices.

SARONA MARKET

Continue north from Bialik, along Tsvi Brock and Bar Kokhkva Streets until the latter intersects with Bograshov Street, a pretty lane of cafés and restaurants. Turn right on Bograshov Street, which eventually becomes Marmorek Street. At the junction with Carlebach Street is the **Tel Aviv Cinémathèque** ⑫, a good place to go for avant-garde and non-English language movies. Ha-Arba'a Street, which runs to the right of the cinémathèque, leads to **Sarona Market** ⑬.

Sarona was a German Templar agricultural colony established in 1871. The land and its buildings were expropriated by the British Mandatory authorities during World War II and after independence the area became part of the Israeli government's Tel Aviv complex of offices. In 2014, the 33 original Templar buildings were renovated and reopened as an outdoor shopping mall and park.

Sarona Market itself opened on the first floor of the adjacent high-rise building and bills itself as an indoor urban culinary market. It is a collection of high-end food and wine stores with an emphasis on expensive, imported products from around the world, as well as the best of the Israeli culinary scene. It's a great place to grab something to eat; although in the indoor market section, due to lack of space, the eateries only have a bar-type arrangement where you sit on stools. Try **Captain Curry** ③, run by one of Israel's best chefs, Johnathan Roshfeld, for a delicious curry.

Scullers in Yarkon Park

NORTH TEL AVIV

*North Tel Aviv is home to the green expanse of Yarkon Park,
bisected by the River Yarkon, and some of the city's best museums.*

DISTANCE: 5km (3 miles)
TIME: Full day
START: Little Old Tel Aviv
END: Museum of the Jewish People
POINTS TO NOTE: To fully appreciate the
River Yarkon and Yarkon Park, this tour is
best done on foot. However, driving and
taking taxis is also an option, especially
if you want to spend more time in the
museums.

Historically, Tel Aviv was always a tale
of north and south, the north synony-
mous with wealth and the south with
poverty.

In recent years, however, many parts
of the south, such as Jaffa and Florentin,
have become affluent and expensive,
although pockets of poverty remain. At
the same time, the north has simply got
richer. Real estate prices in the center
and the Old North (between the center
and the River Yarkon) are among the
most expensive in the world, and they
don't get much cheaper north of the
Yarkon Park, a large swathe of green
along the banks of the River Yarkon.
This is Tel Aviv's equivalent of Central
Park or Hyde Park. North of the river are
streets of expensive apartment buildings, surrounding Tel Aviv University.

LITTLE OLD TEL AVIV

A few minutes' walk inland from Tel Aviv
port is **Little Old Tel Aviv ❶,** which was
the heart of Tel Aviv's nightlife in the
1960s and 70s. The area, at the con-
vergence and northern end of three of
the city's main north–south roads –
Yarkon, Ben Yehuda, and Dizengoff –
remains a trendy neighborhood full of
small bars and restaurants. If you fancy
a filling breakfast first, try **Benedict
❶**, which is a little to the south on Ben
Yehuda Street. Those with a sweet tooth
should head to **Max Brenner ❷**, to the
north on Hata'arucha Road.

When you're ready to continue, go
north on Hata'arucha Street. Just before
the Ben Eliezer Bridge over the River
Yarkon, turn right onto Ussishkin Street
and then descend into the parklands
along the banks of the River Yarkon.

Glass Pavilion at the Eretz Israel Museum

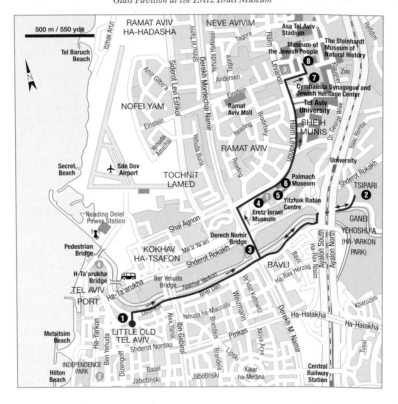

RIVER YARKON

The **River Yarkon** defines the northernmost limit of the city proper, rather than the municipal entity. In biblical times the river marked the border between the tribes of Dan and Ephraim. Today the river is lined with rambling parkland and serves to accommodate scullers who

row along it during the cooler hours of the day. The mouth of the river is to the east, beneath the Reading Power Station, and it stretches east through Yarkon Park and on into Ramat Gan, home of the former national soccer stadium. Swimming is strictly prohibited due to pollution.

If you want to spend more time exploring the river and park (and less time in the

Yitzhak Rabin Center

The Palmach Museum

museums near Tel Aviv University), there are boat rental stations beneath the Ibn Gbriol Street Bridge and the Derekh Namir Bridge. Row boats and pedal boats cost about NIS80 (roughly $20) for an hour, while a motor boat costs NIS200 per hour (roughly $55; one person must be over 21). Tel-O-Fun and Mobike bicycles can be rented here too.

At the eastern end of the park, is the **Tsipari bird sanctuary** ❷ (daily July–Aug 10am–4pm, Sat Sept–June 10am–4pm), a great place for kids with a petting zoo set in lush gardens beside a lake.

Eretz Israel Museum

Cross the river at the **Derech Namir Bridge** ❸ and walk through the park northward to Chaim Levanon Street. At 2 Chaim Levanon Street is the **Eretz Israel Museum** ❹ (tel: 03-641 5244; www.eretzmuseum.org.il; Sat, Mon, Wed 10am–4pm, Tue, Thu 10am–8pm, Fri 10am–2pm; closed Sun). The museum is the region's most comprehensive storehouse of archeological, anthropological, and historical findings. The museum's spiritual backbone is **Tel Kasila**, an excavation site where 12 distinct layers of civilization have been uncovered. The site's finds include an ancient Philistine temple and Hebrew inscriptions from 800 BC. The complex consists of 11 pavilions, including exhibitions of glassware, ceramics, copper, coins, folklore, and ethnography, together with a planetarium. The museum also has an excellent Italian restaurant called **Anina** ❸.

Yitzhak Rabin Center

Practically next door, at 8 Chaim Levanon Street is the **Yitzhak Rabin Center** ❺, (tel: 03-745 3333; www.rabincenter.org.il; Sun, Mon, Wed 9am–3.30pm Tue, Thu 9am–5.30pm, Fri 9am–12.30pm), a library and research center in memory of Israel's assassinated, Prime Minister Yitzhak Rabin. The center, which sits on a hill commanding a panoramic view of Yarkon Park, features a museum telling the story of the State of Israel through Rabin's contribution as a soldier, commander, head of the army, defense minister, prime minister, and peacemaker.

Palmach Museum

Next door again at 10 Chaim Levanon Street is the **Palmach Museum** ❻ (tel: 03-545 9800; make reservation at www.palmach.org.il/english/; Sun–Thu 9am–5pm, Fri 9am–12.30pm; closed Sat), which provides an entertaining multimedia show about the pre-state paramilitary organization, after which the museum is named, who fought fiercely for Israel's independence.

TEL AVIV UNIVERSITY

Farther along Chaim Levanon Street on the right is the entrance to the Tel Aviv University campus. This is the country's largest university and one of its most prestigious. It's pleasant to take a stroll around the campus, although most of the buildings are of no special interest.

Cymbalista Synagogue and Jewish Heritage Center

It is however worth taking a look at the **Cymbalista Synagogue and Jewish Heritage Center** ❼, a striking red-brick faced building designed by the Swiss architect Mario Botta in the 1990s. Its two broad spiralling towers symbolize the Torah scrolls and the need for dialogue between divided parts of society. The interior designs are typically Jewish and universal, with features such as black granite flooring and onyx stone imported from as far afield as Zimbabwe and Pakistan respectively. Nearby is **Japanika** ❹, a great place for Japanese food.

MUSEUM OF THE JEWISH PEOPLE

On the eastern edge of the campus is the **Museum of the Jewish People** ❽ (Bet Hatfutsot; 15 Klausner Street; tel: 03-745 7800; www.bh.org.il; Sun–Wed 10am–5pm, Thu 10am–10pm, Fri 9am–2pm, Sat 10am–3pm). Founded in 1979, it was a departure from conventional museums, telling the story of the Jewish Diaspora rather than simply exhibiting artifacts. The museum underwent a major renovation in 2016, and now boasts cutting-edge technology.

Food and Drink

❶ BENEDICT
171 Ben Yehuda Street; tel: 03-686 8657; daily 24 hrs; $$
This is part of a restaurant chain famous throughout Israel for its hearty breakfasts (served all day), including the distinctly unhealthy English fry-up, complete with strictly non-kosher bacon. This is the place to come if you're tired of that healthy Mediterranean diet.

❷ MAX BRENNER
3 Hata'arucha Street; Tel: 03-544 5480; Sun–Thu 10am–midnight, Fri and Sat 7am–1.30am; $
This is a great place to indulge sweet-toothed children, as the dessert section of the menu is plentiful and chocolate-heavy. For breakfast, there are also healthier salads and eggs, as well as not-so-healthy waffles. By and large, you'll need a sweet tooth and low blood glucose count to enjoy yourself here.

❸ ANINA
2 Chaim Levanon Street; tel: 03-641 2288; daily 8.30am–midnight; $$
This restaurant, located in the Eretz Israel Museum, offers traditional Italian fare, from pizzas to a diverse range of pasta dishes with a creative twist, and at good-value prices.

❹ JAPANIKA
58 Chaim Levanon Street; tel: 03-723 6100; Sun–Thu 11.30am–midnight, Fri–Sat midday–1am; $$
Located by Tel Aviv University, this restaurant is part of a nationwide chain of restaurants, offering popular Japanese dishes, from noodles to sushi, for lunch and dinner.

On the beach in Herzliya

MEDITERRANEAN COAST

*The coast from Tel Aviv to the Lebanese border not only has 128km
(80 miles) of golden beaches but also much history including the ancient
Crusader port of Akko and the Roman capital of Caesarea.*

DISTANCE: 131km (80 miles) each way
TIME: Full day
START: Tel Aviv
END: Rosh Hanikra
POINTS TO NOTE: This is a linear tour that must be done by car. There are plenty of options for overnight stays along the coast, especially in Haifa, if you want to slow the pace down. It might be worth skipping Herzliya and Netanya, the resorts north of Tel Aviv, to spend more time in Caesarea, Haifa, and Akko. When the tour is over, the fastest way to return to Tel Aviv from the north is along the inland Highway 6 toll road, rather than the Coastal Highway.

The crowded city beaches of Tel Aviv are not to everybody's taste. Many visitors have the urge to flee the city for more deserted stretches of sand. This tour is short of no such locations, while some of the best beaches in Israel are included too.

However the Mediterranean coastline is much more than just sea and sand. There is an abundance of history and natural beauty to be found, from the ancient Roman capital of Caesarea and the forests of Mount Carmel, to the beauty of Haifa and the ancient port of Akko, to the grottos of Rosh Hanikra on the Lebanese border.

HERZLIYA AND NETANYA

Herzliya ❶ is home to many of Israel's wealthiest residents. Its stylish beaches and seafront luxury hotels make it a firm favorite with ambassadors and business executives. The most expensive part of the city, Herzliya Pituach, is between the high-tech park and the coast. On the seafront in the north of Herzliya is **Apollonia** (Tel Arshaf) in the **Sidma Ali National Park** (daily 8am–5pm; free), an ancient site comprising the ruins of a Hellenistic city and a Crusader fortress.

Some 22km (13 miles) farther north is the city of **Netanya ❷**, the capital city of the Sharon region. Originally founded as a citrus colony in 1929, Netanya has – if you'll excuse the pun – blossomed: it has an attractive beach and prome-

Roman ruins at Caesarea

nade, including a striking glass elevator down to the beach just south of the city center to help the infirm negotiate the high cliffs. Netanya has a population of 240,000 and a galaxy of budget-priced hotels clustered along the beachfront. The Tourist Information Office (Sun–Thu 9am–5pm) is in Independence Square near the seafront.

Mikhmoret Beach

Several kilometres north of Netanya is **Mikhmoret Beach ❸**, beautiful and seldom crowded. Here you can find sandy coves to nestle in and extraordinary sunsets from atop the cliffs and if you are lucky you might stumble across the local population of large sea turtles. The beach is free but you'll need to pay for parking.

CAESAREA

Caesarea ❹ (daily 8am–4pm, until 5pm Mar–Sept), built by Herod, was once the Roman capital of Judea province. However it is the Crusader ruins that really catch the eye. Entry to the **Crusader City** is through a vaulted gatehouse and bridge over a wide moat. The walls around the city, which slope down precipitously from an imposing height, are the city's most awe-inspiring monument. Along the waterfront, Roman pillars used as foundation stones by the Crusaders jut out among the waves. There is also a Byzantine street of statues and the restored **Roman Amphitheater**, a stirring venue

for concerts overlooking the Mediterranean. Inland from the ruins is one of the few golf courses in Israel. If you're hungry, head to Caesarea port, where there are many good places to eat, including **Limani Bistro ❶**.

ZIKHRON YA'AKOV

A little over 10km (6 miles) farther north along the coast is the beginning of the Carmel Mountain Range. Shortly afterward is the town of **Zikhron Ya'akov ❺**, which was established in 1882 in memory of James Rothschild. Just south of the quaint 19th century cobblestone town center is **Rothschild's Tomb**, built in the 1950s to house the remains of the Parisian banker and his wife Adelaide. The tomb is located amid a fragrant garden (Yad Hanadiv) of date trees, sage, roses, and other flowers.

MOUNT CARMEL NATIONAL PARK

Before reaching Haifa to the east is **Mount Carmel National Park ❻** (always open), Israel's largest national forest preserve, with deer and gazelle roaming freely in the lush hilly woodlands. An extra fee is charged for entering the **Khai Bar Nature Reserve** (daily 8am–3pm), where rare fallow deer from Iran, previously extinct in this region, have been reintroduced. Tucked among the slopes and valleys of the Carmel Range, are the Druze villages of **Daliyat el-Karmel** and **Isfiya ❼**.

Cable car, Haifa

HAIFA

On the gentle slopes of Mount Carmel is **Haifa**, Israel's third-largest city, which is a high-tech hub and a busy port city. Haifa is also home to the Technion, Israel's oldest university.

Along the seafront

Most of Haifa's **best beaches 8** are at the southern entrance to the city. Farther along before the central part of the city, at the start of Haifa Bay, is **Bat Galim Beach 9**, the only beach in the country facing north, which is perfect for surfing.

Opposite the monastery, a platform marks the upper terminal of **Haifa's cable car** (daily 9am–11pm, closed Fri in winter), which ferries passengers from the Carmel down to the Bat Galim

Bahá'í Hillside Gardens

Promenade. Thanks to the shape of Israel's coastline, Haifa has some glorious beaches. There is a cable-car from the beach here, going up to the **Carmelite Monastery 10** (daily 6am–1.30pm, 3–6pm), the world center of the Carmelite Order. The site was selected in the 12th century by Crusaders and the church was built in the 18th century, over a grotto associated with the prophet Elijah and his disciple Elisha. **Elijah's Cave** (Sun–Thu 8am–5pm; free) can be reached by a footpath from the monastery. The prophet is said to have meditated here in the 9th century BC.

German Colony

Back down on the coast, the main highway leads in to the **German Colony 11**, one of the most attractive parts of Haifa. Built in 1868 by the German Templars, this area has become gentrified in recent years with the restoration of delightful old houses and gardens and the addition of a cluster of several excellent restaurants along Ben Gurion Avenue, including **Fattoush 2**. The beauty of the German Colony has been further accentuated by the recently completed **Bahá'í Hillside Gardens** (see box) **12**, rising majestically up the hill, with the gold-domed Bahá'í Shrine at their peak.

Drive up Mount Carmel to the **Carmel Center 13** for panoramic vistas of the city, sea, and mountains. Atop the crest of Mount Carmel is the **University of Haifa 14**, its distinctive 25-floor tower thrusting resolutely against the

German Colony in Haifa

Akko's port

sky, offering an unparalleled view of northern Israel.

From the university continue along Highway 705 and down the Carmel Mountain past Nesher – a nondescript suburb of Haifa – and then take Road 22 north along Haifa Bay, and on to Akko.

AKKO

Akko ⓑ (also called Acre) is one of the world's oldest ports, mentioned by the Pharaohs in 1500 BC and captured by the Egyptians in 261 BC; Alexander the Great and Julius Caesar both passed through Akko too. It was chosen as the key port of the Crusader Kingdom by Baldwin I in 1104, before falling to the Mamelukes in 1291. The Ottomans defeated Napoleon here, but with the establishment of a deeper port in nearby Haifa, the city soon sank into obscurity. In 2001, Unesco declared Old Akko a World Heritage Site.

The city walls and dry moats were both built by the Crusaders. Near the entrance to the **Old Akko** is the Visitors' Center (daily 8.30am–5pm, until 6pm in summer), where you'll want to start. Nearby is the northeastern command post, with a strategic view and a restored promenade, which continues on to Land Gate, and on to the bay. In the Old City, the first prominent structure is the elegant **el-Jazzar Mosque** (open dawn to dusk), built in 1781–82, and one of the largest mosques in the Holy Land.

The Bahá'í Hillside Gardens

Dominating Haifa's Mount Carmel hillside is the Bahá'í complex, which includes the world's longest hillside gardens, as well as the golden-domed Bahá'í shrine and the palatial Seat of the Universal House of Justice (Bahá'í World Headquarters).

The centerpiece is the golden-domed Shrine of the Bab, which contains the tomb of Siyyad Ali Muhammed – the Bab – a Persian Muslim who proclaimed the coming of a 'Promised One' in 1844. He was executed for heresy in 1850, and his disciples brought his remains to Haifa in 1909.

Haifa became the center of Bahá'í activity when the 'Promised One' – Husayn-Ali, Baha'u'llah – settled in Palestine. He is buried near Akko where he died in 1892. Baha'u'llah's son, Abbas Effendi, instructed believers to purchase large tracts of Mount Carmel overlooking Haifa Bay.

Extending from the summit of Mount Carmel, this unique hillside terraced garden, which was completed in 2001, spreads out spectacularly along the northwest slope of the mountain.

The Shrine of the Bab and the Bahá'í Gardens are open to the public, free of charge. However, guided tours must be reserved at least 24 hours in advance (tel: 04-831 3131).

A tunnel at Akko's Crusader City

Nearby is the towering **Citadel and Museum of Heroism** (Sat–Thu 9.30am–5pm, Fri 9.30am–noon). Built on Crusader ruins, the fortress was used variously as an arsenal, a barracks and, since Turkish times, as a prison. This was where Jewish underground fighters were executed during the British Mandate. Abutting the Citadel is the dank subterranean **Crusader City** (Sat–Thu 9am–4.30pm, Fri 9am–12.30pm).

As you emerge from the subterranean city, there is a restored Turkish bathhouse, which is now the **Municipal Museum** (same hours as Crusader City; tickets valid for both). The museum contains exhibits on archeology, Islamic culture, folklore, and weaponry. Farther in is the Greek Orthodox St George's Church, dedicated to two British officers who fell at Akko in 1799 and 1840. Of special interest are the *khans* (inns) that grace the portside area, including the imposing Khan el-Afranj (Inn of the Franks), near the Bazaar, and the Khan el-Umdan (Inn of the Pillars). Close by too, is the **Doniana** ❸, one of the best places to eat in Akko.

Continuing north from Akko, past the resort town of Nahariya, the road comes to an end near the Lebanese border at **Rosh ha-Nikra** ⑯, where there are attractive grottoes, formed by millennia of erosion from the sea. A cable car (www.rosh-hanikra.com; daily 8.30am–4pm, until Apr–mid-July and mid-Aug–Sept, until midnight) goes down over the pounding tide; there is also a footpath for the determined. The cliff is the southernmost edge of the Ladder of Tyre Mountain Range and offers a view over a now walled-up railroad tunnel that once led to Lebanon.

Food and Drink

❶ LIMANI BISTRO

Caesarea Port; tel: 04-610 0022; open daily noon–11pm; $$

Limani is a fish restaurant in a delightful location, overlooking Caesarea's old Crusader port, and serving the usual selection of delicious Eastern Mediterranean fish and salads.

❷ FATTOUSH

38 Ben Gurion Avenue, German Colony, Haifa; tel: 04-852 4930; daily 11am–midnight; $$

One of several excellent restaurants in Haifa's German Colony, Fattoush serves a diverse array of creative Middle Eastern dishes for both vegetarians and meat-eaters.

❸ DONIANA

Salah Al-Batzri Street, Pizani Harbour, Akko, next to the lighthouse; tel: 04-991 0001; daily 11am–11pm; $$

Overlooking the Mediterranean near ancient Akko port, Doniana is the pick of the city's restaurants, and specializes in fish and seafood. Also serves tasty salads and dips.

On the Sea of Galilee

THE GALILEE

Under two hours by car from Tel Aviv, the Galilee is of profound significance to Christians and Jews. History and religion aside, it is also an attractive region, full of mountains, valleys, and streams feeding the Sea of Galilee.

DISTANCE: 200km (125 miles) each way, with a return journey of 167km (104 miles)
TIME: Full day
START: Tel Aviv
END: Tiberias/Beit She'an
POINTS TO NOTE: This tour must be undertaken by car. There are plenty of options for overnight stays in the Galilee, should you wish to extend your stay and take the sightseeing at your own pace, and also extending it to locations not mentioned in this tour, such as the Golan Heights. It may be over-ambitious to visit all the sites on this route in one day, unless you set out from Tel Aviv at 6am and return late at night, so use your own discretion. Nazareth, Safed, the Sea of Galilee, and Tiberias are the most important places to visit.

The Galilee, just 90 or so minutes by car from Tel Aviv, is redolent with religious significance: Jesus was born in Bethlehem and died in Jerusalem, but the Galilee is where he lived and preached. The region is also of major importance to Jews. The Galilee town of Tiberias was where much of the rabbinical Talmudic commentary of the Old Testament was written; while the Safed is associated with the mystical Kabbalah.

Even without this sacred history, the Galilee would be an attractive region. Biblical prominence may have exaggerated the size of the River Jordan, which is just a broad stream, and the Sea of Galilee, not a sea, but an inland lake, but they are attractive nonetheless. Despite the southerly latitude, the Galilee hillsides in spring are ablaze with flowers and as green as anywhere in Northern Europe as the land is fed by the melting snow of majestic Mount Hermon and the Golan Heights.

Drive north out of Tel Aviv and east along Highway 5 until the intersection with Highway 6, and then head north. Drive along Highway 6 until the Iron Interchange and then head east along Highway 65. Alternatively, if you want

Tel Megiddo

to avoid the toll on Road 6, which is charged automatically with some rental companies often adding an additional handling fee, it will take 15–30 minutes longer to travel along the coastal highway. If you take this detour, turn onto Highway 65 after Hadera, which leads through Wadi Ara before opening out into the Jezreel Valley.

TEL MEGIDDO

About 29km (18 miles) from the Iron Interchange is the Megiddo Junction. North from here, along Highway 66, is **Tel Megiddo ❶** (daily 8am–4pm, until 5pm Apr–Sept), a 4,000-year-old city made famous by the Book of Revelation as the site for mankind's final battle at Armageddon. Archeologists have uncovered 20 cities here, including a 4,000-year-old Canaanite temple, King Solomon's stables, and an underground water system built by King Ahab 2,800 years ago.

NAZARETH

Return to Highway 65 and continue east and then north on 60 to **Nazareth ❷**, the quaint village where Jesus grew up that has become one of the world's best-known towns. Today Nazareth is a bustling city of 80,000, Israel's largest Arab city, with almost two dozen churches commemorating its most esteemed resident. The grandest of all is the monumental **Church of the Annunciation** (Mon–Sat 8am–6pm, until 5pm in winter, Sun 2–5pm; free). The largest church in the Middle East, it was completed in 1969, encompassing the remains of previous Byzantine churches, marking the spot where the Angel Gabriel is said to have informed the Virgin Mary that God had chosen her to bear His son. **Tishreen ❶**, serving excellent Mediterranean and Middle-Eastern dishes, is located close by the Church of the Annunciation.

In the basement of the **Church of St Joseph** (next to the Basilica) is a cavern reputed to have been the carpentry workshop of Joseph, Jesus's earthly father. Some of the simpler churches, however, capture an air of intimacy and sanctity that the colossal Basilica lacks. This is especially so in the **Greek Orthodox Church of St Gabriel,** nearly a kilometre (0.6 mile) farther north.

Return to Highway 60 and go south. Near Afula turn eastward on Highway 65 to **Mount Tabor ❸**, which rises to the east of Nazareth offering a panorama of the whole Jezreel Valley. It was here that the biblical prophetess Deborah was said to have led an army of 10,000 Israelites to defeat their idol-worshipping enemies. Two churches commemorate the transfiguration of Christ, which is believed to have taken place here. The Franciscan **Basilica of the Transfiguration** commemorates the event, which Christians believe foreshadowed his resurrection.

Prayers in the Church of the Annunciation, Nazareth

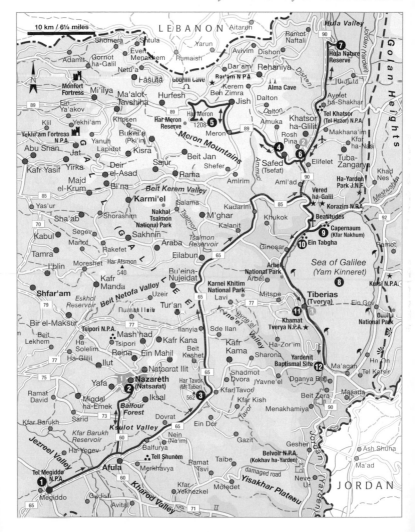

Gallery in Safed

MYSTICAL SAFED

A further 66km (41 miles) north along Highways 65, 85, 90, and finally 89 is **Safed** ❹, an attractive hilltop town where narrow, cobblestone streets wind their way through stone archways and overlook the domed rooftops of 16th-century houses and medieval synagogues. Legend has it that part of the mystical Kabbalah was written here.

The rabbinical scholars of Safed were so prolific that in 1563 the city set up the first printing press in Asia. Not all the synagogues here are medieval, many of the original ones having been destroyed and replaced by more modern structures, but the spirit of the old still lingers in these few lanes off Kikar Meginim. The special atmosphere that permeates Safed has captured the imagination of dozens of artists who have made it their home and set up an artists' colony alongside the synagogues. Towering above the center of Safed, littered with Crusader ruins, is **Citadel Hill**, an excellent lookout point, taking in an excellent panorama that extends from the slopes of Lebanon to the Sea of Galilee.

If you are staying overnight in the Galilee, you may wish to consider a detour farther north, along Highway 886 and 89 to **Mount Meron** ❺. At 1,208 meters (3,963ft), Mount Meron is the highest peak in the Galilee, with a sweeping view from the Mediterranean to Mount Hermon. These mountains are filled with the mystery of the tombs of the rabbis, such as Shimon Bar-Yochai, who composed the Kabbalah, in **Meron** village.

The Galilee Panhandle

Backtrack to Safed. To the east is the town of **Rosh Pina** ❻, which is in the Galilee Panhandle, a thin strip of Israel surrounded by Lebanon and Syria. Rosh Pina was first settled by Russian Jewish families in the 1880s. Cobblestone streets line the old section of the town, together with gentrified 19th-century houses. If you're hungry, stop off at **Pina Barosh – Shiri Bistro** ❷ for a delicious lunch with an even better view.

Also in the Galilee Panhandle is the **Hula Valley**, part of the Syrian-African Rift Valley, which was formerly a malaria-infested swamp. By 1957 the lake had been emptied, leaving a verdant valley in its place. However, part of the region has now been re-swamped, as excessive peat in the ground is impeding agriculture. You can get an idea of what the area was like before the drainage by visiting the 80 hectares (200 acres) of swamp land that have been set aside as the **Hula Nature Reserve** ❼ (Sat–Thu 8am–4pm, Fri 8am–3pm).

SEA OF GALILEE

Head back south on Highway 90 and soon you will see the **Sea of Galilee** ❽ glowing like an emerald, its tranquil surface framed in a purplish-brown halo of mountains. The Sea of Galilee is in fact a lake just 21km (13 miles) long and 11km

Birdwatching at Hula Lake   *Greek Orthodox Church at Capernaum*

(7 miles) wide. It may not be enormous by global standards, but it has, through some romantically inspired hyperbole, come to be known as a 'sea'. In Hebrew it is called Yam Kinneret, because it's shaped like a *kinnor* or harp.

These bountiful shores have been inhabited for millennia, with the earliest evidence of habitation dating back 5,000 years to a cult of moon-worshippers that sprouted in the south. Some 3,000 years later the lake witnessed the birth and spread of Christianity on its shores, while high up on the cliffs above, Jewish rebels sought refuge from Roman soldiers. The dramas of the past, however, have since faded into the idyllic landscape.

Monastery of the Beatitudes

On a hilltop along Highway 90 overlooking the Sea of Galilee to the north is where it is believed that Jesus proclaimed to the masses that had gathered below: "Blessed are the meek, for they shall inherit the earth". This well-known line from the Sermon on the Mount is immortalized by the majestic **Church and Monastery of the Beatitudes** ❽ (daily 8am–5pm; free). An octagonal church, it is set in well-maintained gardens, and belongs to the Franciscan order and was built in the 1930s.

CAPERNAUM

It was in the fishing villages around the northern edge of the Sea of Galilee

below that Jesus found his first followers. The village of **Capernaum** ❾ on the northern tip of the lake became his second home. Here he is said to have preached more sermons and performed more miracles than anywhere else.

It was a metropolis of sorts in its heyday, and at least five of the disciples came from here. It is after one of them, a simple fisherman named Peter, that the Galilee's most renowned fish, the St Peter's fish, is named. Today the site houses the elaborate remains of a 2nd-century synagogue, said to be built over the original one where Jesus used to preach. There is also a recently completed church, shaped like a ship, on what was believed to be the house of St Peter, a Franciscan Monastery, and the colorful red domed roofs of the Greek Orthodox Church of the Seven Apostles.

Remains of a synagogue in Capernaum

Tiberias

Ein Tabgha

In the neighboring town of **Ein Tabgha** ⑩, Jesus is said to have multiplied five loaves and two fishes into enough food to feed the 5,000 hungry people who had come to hear him preach. The modern **Church of the Multiplication** (daily 8.30am–5pm) was constructed over the colorful mosaic floor of a Byzantine shrine in 1982. Next to it stands the Church of Peter's Primacy.

TIBERIAS

The capital of the lake, **Tiberias** ⑪, is a sprawling city of 60,000 located halfway down the west coast, and one of the country's most popular resorts. Its boardwalk is lined with excellent seafood restaurants, such as **Decks Restaurant** ③, where you can sample some delicious St Peter's fish while enjoying a stunning view of the lake. On the marina you can have your pick of water-skiing or windsurfing, or go for a dip at one of the beaches along the outskirts of the city.

Tiberias is considered one of the four holy Jewish cities, and is home to the tombs of famous Jewish sages, including the 12th-century philosopher Moses Maimonides and the self-taught scholar, Rabbi Akiva, who was killed by the Romans after the Bar-Kochba Uprising. Tiberias was founded by Herod Antipas around AD 20 because of its hot springs. In the 2nd and 3rd centuries Jewish scholars codified the sounds of the Hebrew script and wrote the Mishnah, the great commentary on the Bible.

Spa treatments

Today the mineral-rich **hot springs,** just south of the city center remain a major drawing card. The original baths the Romans used are exhibited in the **National Archeological Park** across the street in a fascinating little **museum** (Sun–Thu 10am–noon, 3–5pm). Nearby archeologists have uncovered a 2nd-century mosaic synagogue floor; Maimonides' tomb on Ben Zakai Street, just south of the hotel district, is a popular site for Jewish pilgrims.

If you aren't staying in the Galilee overnight, chances are you'll want to think about heading back to Tel Aviv now, via Highways 77 and then 6 (toll road) or on Highway 2, which should take around two hours.

Baptism in the Jordan

Continue south on Highway 90, which skirts the western shore of the Sea of Galilee. Shortly after Jesus left Nazareth at the age of 30, he met John the Baptist preaching near the waters of the Jordan. It was here, in the river that the Bible so often describes as a boundary – and, more figuratively, as a point of transition – that Jesus was baptized. Once cleansed, he set out on his mission. One tradition holds that the baptism took place at the point where the Sea of Galilee merges with the Jordan River near what is today **Kibbutz Kinneret,** 12km (8 miles) south of Tiberias.

The promenade, Tiberias   *The Roman ampitheater at Beit She'an*

The **Yardenit Baptismal Site** ⑫ (Sat–Thu 8am–5pm, Fri 8am–4pm) has been established just outside the kibbutz in order to accommodate the many pilgrims who still converge on the spot. There is also a rival baptismal site further south, near Jericho.

Around the point where the lake merges with the Jordan River in the south are the three oldest kibbutzim: **Dganya Alef**, **Dganya Bet** and **Kinneret £**. Kinneret's cemetery, on the lakeside is the burial place for leading Israeli figures and is a marvellous place for tranquil contemplation.

BEIT SHE'AN

Farther southwest along Road 90 is the ancient *tel* (a place that has been inhab-ited for thousands of years, often with layers built over one another) of **Beit She'an**, reflecting 6,000 years of civilization. In the **Beit She'an National Park** (daily 8am–4pm, until 8pm Apr–Sept) sits Israel's best-preserved Roman theater, which once seated 8,000, and an archeological museum featuring a Byzantine mosaic floor. Beit She'an was once part of the Roman Decapolis – the ten most important cities in the Eastern Mediterranean. Also here are a colonnaded street, and a ruined temple that collapsed in an 8th century earthquake.

To the east of the modern town is the **Jordan River Crossing**, which will take you to Jordan; to the west Highways 60, 65 and then 6, or 2, will take you back to Tel Aviv.

Food and Drink

① TISHREEN
56 El-Bishara Street, near Mary's Well, Nazareth; tel: 04-608 4666; daily 11am–11pm; $$
This restaurant near the Church of the Annunciation offers traditional Middle East and Mediterranean fare. Specialty dishes include Arab pizza topped with chicken, and aubergine stuffed with pesto.

② PINA BAROSH – SHIRI BISTRO
8 HaChalutzim Street, Rosh Pina; tel: 04-693 6852; daily 8.30am–11pm; $$
Delightfully located in the 19th-century village of Rosh Pina, overlooking the Hula Valley and Mount Hermon beyond, this steak restaurant serves excellent meat dishes and salads.

③ DECKS RESTAURANT
13 Gdud Barak Street, Tiberias; tel 04-671 0800; noon–11pm; $$
This restaurant provides a perfect opportunity to eat the biblical St Peter's fish (*tilapia*) while looking out over the Sea of Galilee. The restaurant also serves excellent steaks and has vegetarian dishes.

DIRECTORY

Hand-picked hotels and restaurants to suit all budgets and tastes, organised by area, plus select nightlife listings, an alphabetical listing of practical information, a language guide and an overview of the best books and films to give you a flavor of the region.

Suite at the American Colony

ACCOMMODATIONS

There is a wide choice of accommodations in Jerusalem and Tel Aviv, although prices are relatively expensive, ranging from hundreds of dollars per night in high-end hotels to $50 per night in a respectable hostel. Unique Israeli forms of accommodations include kibbutz guesthouses (relatively expensive rural retreats) and Christian hospices, more luxurious than they sound, usually with a 19th-century European ambiance, and not to be confused with hospitals for the terminally ill. Both of these offer an unusual taste of Israel. Youth hostels range from hole-in-the-wall downtown joints, through to the facilities of the Israel Youth Hostel Association, which are usually well-appointed, and of three-star hotel quality (with prices to match). Then there is also Airbnb, which can offer the best value, as well as websites like Booking.com. Prices are usually far cheaper when booked as part of a package in advance.

In Jerusalem, prices are heavily influenced by location, with hotels overlooking the Old City walls being the most expensive, and hotels farther away from

the city center much cheaper. Generally speaking, hotels in Arab East Jerusalem offer better value than hotels in Jewish West Jerusalem. Visitors may want to consider staying in one of the hotels in the Jerusalem hills (many of them kibbutzim), which are just a short drive from the city and 30 minutes from Tel Aviv. Accommodations in the village of Ein Kerem, officially within Jerusalem's municipal boundaries, provide a delightful rural retreat, yet are close to the city center.

In Tel Aviv, the seafront is one long strip of high-rise hotels overlooking the beaches. Jaffa and the inland business district have many boutique hotels, which can be far more expensive than seafront hotels as they cater for businesspeople rather than vacationers. Holidaymakers deterred by the pace of life in Tel Aviv may prefer the exclusive, but also expensive, tourist resort of Herzliya, north of Tel Aviv.

Jerusalem
Addar
53 Nablus Road; tel: 02-626 3111. www.addar-hotel.com; $

This is a relatively new and comfortable, good-value Arab hotel with a warm, cosy atmosphere in a well-appointed building opposite St George's Cathedral and near the Damascus Gate and Garden Tomb.

> $ Up to $100 per night
> $$ $101–200 per night
> $$$ $201–300 per night
> $$$$ $301–400 per night

Courtyard garden at the American Colony

Arthur

13 Dorot Rishonim Street; tel: 02-623 9999; www.atlas.co.il/arthur-jerusalem; $$$
This is a recently opened boutique hotel in the heart of downtown Jerusalem's traffic-free area, within easy walking distance of the Old City and Makhanei Yehuda market. The hotel prides itself on its Israeli-style breakfasts, warm atmosphere, and retro-modern decor.

American Colony

1 Louis Vincent Street, off Nablus Road; tel: 02-627 9777; www.americancolony.com; $$$
Jerusalem's oldest hotel (not counting hospices) was established in 1881 by a Christian family. With its gourmet restaurants, landscaped gardens, stylish outdoor pool, and high-tech fitness room, the hotel has much character and charm and is favored by foreign journalists on account of its neutral location between West and East Jerusalem.

Austrian Hospice

37 Via Dolorosa, tel: 02-626 5800; www.austrianhospice.com; $$
This grand and ornate 19th-century building on the Via Dolorosa served as a hospital for many years but was renovated in the late 1980s. The Austrian Hospice is an oasis of serenity amid the hubbub of the Old City – don't miss its authentic Viennese coffee house and central European cuisine, with schnitzel, goulash, and strudel.

Christmas

Ali Ibn Abi Taleb Street; tel: 02-628 2588; www.christmas-hotel.com; $
This is an attractive small boutique Arab hotel in the heart of East Jerusalem with a delightful garden, attractive decor, comfortable rooms, and warm personal service.

Dan Jerusalem

32 Lekhi, Mount Scopus; tel: 02-533 1234; www3.danhotels.com/JerusalemHotels/DanJerusalemHotel; $$
With its stylish exteriors and interiors, outdoor patios, and swimming pool, this large hotel sits atop Mount Scopus near the Hebrew University, far from the bustle of the city, and commands a breathtaking view of the Old City.

David's Citadel

7 David ha-Melekh, Jerusalem; tel: 02-621 1111. www.thedavidcitadel.com; $$$$
This luxury hotel, attractively designed and superbly appointed, is by the Mamilla Mall near the Jaffa Gate and downtown Jerusalem and has stirring views of the Old City walls.

Holiday Inn Crowne Plaza

Givat Ram; tel: 02-658 8888; www.ihg.com/crowneplaza/hotels/gb/en/jerusalem; $$
This landmark high-rise building at the western entrance to the city, opposite the Central Bus Station and new train station, offers luxury accommodations for modest prices and is convenient for touring locations outside of the city.

Lobby at the King David Hotel

Inbal

3 Jabotinski; tel: 02-675 6666; www.
inbalhotel.com; $$$

Overlooking the Liberty Bell Garden and
Montefiore's windmill, this delightfully
designed hotel, with an attractive central
inner courtyard, has attracted some world
leaders away from the nearby King David.

King David Hotel

23 David ha-Melekh; tel: 02-620 8888;
www3.danhotels.com/JerusalemHotels/
KingDavidJerusalemHotel; $$$$

Israel's premier hotel, and a favorite
among political leaders and the rich and
famous, the King David has style and an
old-world ambiance, beautiful gardens,
and a swimming pool overlooking the
Old City. In terms of service, it doesn't try
quite as hard as some of its newer rivals.

Little House in Baka

1 Yehuda Street, off Hebron Road; tel: 02-
673 7944; $$.

These accommodations are a cross
between a boutique hotel and a guesthouse, in a large, stylish 1920s home in
Jerusalem's trendy Baka neighborhood.

Mamilla Hotel

11 Solomon Hamelekh Street; tel: 02-548
2222; www.mamillahotel.com; $$$$

One of Jerusalem's newest hotels is also
one of the city's most luxurious and, inev-
itably, most expensive. Best of all, the
hotel is above the newly opened Mamilla
shopping mall and adjacent to the Old
City walls, with breathtaking views.

Mount Zion

17 Hebron Road; tel: 02-5689 555; www.
mountzion-jerusalem.com; $$

Originally an ophthalmology hospital, built
more than a century ago, this building was
converted into a stylish and ornate luxury
hotel overlooking the Old City walls.

Notre Dame

3 Hatsanhanim Street; tel: 02-627 9111;
https://www.notredamecenter.org/; $$$

Notre Dame offers luxurious accommodations, splendid 19th-century architecture and one of Jerusalem's best
(non-kosher) restaurants. It's a superbly
appointed hospice, opposite the Old City
walls and the New Gate. Vatican-owned,
it has been extensively renovated and
demonstrates that pilgrims in the 19th
century knew how to enjoy life.

Orient Jerusalem

3 Emek Refaim Street; tel: 02-569 9090;
www.isrotel.com/orient; $$$

One of the city's most recently opened
hotels is located in the German Colony
opposite the old train station and within
comfortable walking distance of the
Old City and downtown Jerusalem. The
decor is delightful and the hotel has a
rooftop infinity pool.

Our Sisters of Zion

Ein Kerem; tel: 02-641 5738; http://www.
notredamedesion.org/centres/ein-kerem-
guest-house/; $$

Delightful Provençal-style pension,
located in Ein Kerem, with spacious gar-

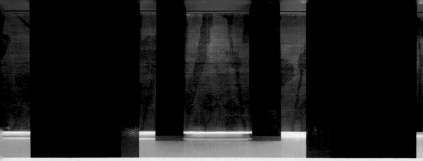

dens filled with olive trees and grape vines. Comfortable accommodations.

Palatin Hotel

4 Agrippas Street; tel: 02-623 1141; www. palatinhotel.com; $$
A clean and comfortable hotel in a central location in West Jerusalem, the Palatin is close to the Makhane Yehuda market.

Prima Palace

6 Pines Street; tel: 02-531 1811; www. prima-hotels-israel.com/PalaceHotel/ Jerusalem; $$
The Prima Palace is a colorful ultra-Orthodox establishment in the heart of West Jerusalem, which provides an opportunity to observe the customs of the most religious Jewish communities.

Ramat Rachel Hotel and Spa

Kibbutz Ramat Rachel; tel: 02-670 2555; www.ramatrachel.co.il; $$
Although within the city limits, the kibbutz grounds offer a stirring view of the Judean Desert. It offers comfortable accommodations, and the kibbutz is adjacent to an unusual olive garden.

Scots Guesthouse

St Andrews Church, 1 David Remez Street; tel: 02-673 2401; www.scotsguesthouse. com; $$
Intimate guesthouse atmosphere, in central location by the old train station. No kippers, but there is sometimes haggis as well as mince pies and mulled wine at Christmas, and always whisky.

YMCA 3 Arches Hotel

26 David Ha-Melekh; tel: 02-569 2652; www.ymca3arches.com; $$
Stylish 1930s building opposite the King David Hotel; designed by the same architect who planned the Empire State Building.

Jerusalem Hills

Cramim Resort & Spa Hotel

Kibbutz Kiryat Anavim, Judean Hills; tel: 02-548 9800; www.isrotelexclusivecollection. com/cramim; $$$$
This luxury hotel is surrounded by vineyards, forests, and hiking trails and is just a 15-minute drive from Jerusalem and just over 30 minutes to Tel Aviv.

Yearim Hotel

Kibbutz Ma'aleh Hahamisha; tel: 02-533 1331; https://eng.yearimhotel.com; $$
High in the Jerusalem hills on a mountain peak, the hotel offers breathtaking panoramas, bracing country walks in the forest, and comfortable accommodations close to both Jerusalem and Tel Aviv.

Tel Aviv and Jaffa

Cinema

2 Zamenhoff, Dizengoff Circle; tel: 03-520 7100. www.cinemahotel.com; $$
In the heart of Tel Aviv's café district, this 80-room hotel is in a converted movie theater and is one of the city's finest examples of Bauhaus architecture.

City

9 Mapu Street; tel: 03-524 6253; www. atlashotels.co.il; $

Near the beach and city center, this clean and comfortable hotel puts a roof over your head at a reasonable price.

Crowne Plaza Hotel

132 Menachem Begin Road; tel: 03-777 4000; www.ihg.com/crowneplaza/hotels/us/en/tel-aviv/tlvcc/hoteldetail; $$$

Located on the upper floors of the iconic Azrieli Center, this hotel offers splendid views of the city and is aimed at businesspeople rather than beach lovers, with only a distant view of the sea.

Dan Tel Aviv

99 Ha-Yarkon; tel: 03-520 2525; www.danhotels.com; $$$

The city's veteran luxury hotel offers excellent sea views and is renowned for comfort, style, and convenience.

David Intercontinental

12 Kaufman Street; tel: 03-7951 111; www.ihg.com/intercontinental/hotels/us/en/tel-aviv/tlvha/hoteldetail; $$

This is one of the city's largest and most expensive hotels and often hosts major business conferences and delegations. Overlooking the Mediterranean to the south of Tel Aviv, near Jaffa, the hotel is in the fascinating 19th-century Neve Tzedek neighborhood.

Fabric Hotel

28 Nahlat Binyamin; tel: 03-542 5555; www.atlas.co.il/fabric-hotel/; $$

The hotel, on the site of a former fabrics factory, contains a garden in a hidden courtyard and a hydroponic garden on its roof with a view of Tel Aviv's century-old original neighborhoods.

Gordon Inn

77 Ben Yehuda Street; tel 03-523 8239; www.hostelstelaviv.com; $

This hostel offers basic but clean bed-and-breakfast accommodations, very close to the seafront, with both shared rooms and private rooms and a laid-back atmosphere.

Idelson Hotel

13 Idelson Street; tel: 050-646 3947; www.idelson-hotel.telavivhotelsisrael.com/en/; $

A small and unexceptional hotel not far from the beach and the city center, offering an inexpensive base whilst in town.

Lighthouse

1 Ben Yehuda Street; tell: 03-766 0500; www.brownhotels.com/lighthouse; $$

This stylish boutique hotel is located in a rather unstylish high-rise building, one block from the beach.

Market House Hotel

5 Beit Eshel Street; Jaffa; tel: 03-797 4000; https://www.atlas.co.il/market-house-hotel-tel-aviv-israel; $$

This boutique hotel is located next to Jaffa's historic Clock Tower and renowned flea market, and takes inspiration from the unique and authentic atmosphere of ancient Jaffa.

Suite at the Norman

Montefiore

36 Montefiore Street, Tel Aviv; tel: 03-564 6100; $$$$

Located in a 1920s building this really is a boutique hotel in the best sense of the word, with just 12 rooms. It is far from the sea, but if you can afford the hotel you can probably afford the taxi to the beach.

Norman

23–25 Nahmani Street; tel: 03-543 5555; $$$$

World-class hotel in restored early 20th century buildings, the Norman is a byword for class and style and the place where the wealthiest visitors to the city stay.

Tel Aviv Hilton

205 Hayarkon Street; tel: 03-520 2222. www3.hilton.com/en/hotels/israel/hilton-tel-aviv-TLVHITW/index.html; $$$

One of the city's most luxurious and fashionable hotels with Tel Aviv high society, and prices to match. It's one minute from the beach thanks to its cliff-top location, and has a saltwater pool too.

Herzliya

Dan Accadia

122 Ramot Yam Street; tel: 09-959 7070. www3.danhotels.com/HerzliyaHotels/DanAccadiaHerzliyaHotel; $$$$

Perched on a cliff overlooking the Mediterranean, this is one of Israel's oldest and most elegant luxury hotels, and the pick of the accommodations in this upscale resort to the north of Tel Aviv. The hotel has a great restaurant, spa, and sport amenities on its grounds.

Daniel Herzliya Hotel

60 Ramot Yam Street; tel: 09-952 0808. www.tamareshotels.com/daniel-herzliya-hotel; $$$

This hotel also offers luxury on the seafront, with no expense spared on the meticulously designed palatial decor.

Eshel

3 Ramot Yam Street; tel: 09-956 8208. www.hotels-of-israel.com/eshel/eshel_hotel_herzliya.htm; $$

This hotel provides very modest accommodations in an upscale resort with 36 rooms across the road from the seafront.

Sharon Beach Resort & Spa

4 Ramot Yam Street; tel: 09-952 5777. www.sharon.co.il; $$$

The best value of Herzliya's salubrious seafront hotels, overlooking the Mediterranean and the beach. It also has excellent spa amenities.

Shefayim Kibbutz Guesthouse

Kibbutz Shefayim; tel: 09-959 5577. www.shefhotel.co.il; $$

The closest kibbutz hotel to Tel Aviv is just north of Herzliya and offers an excellent base close to the city and for touring the north of the country. It's also home to Israel's largest water park.

RESTAURANTS

Israel's restaurants reflect the varied multicultural composition of the country. A city center eatery offering mezze salad followed by a meat or fish main course and sweet pastry dessert should cost no more than NIS 150 ($40). Middle Eastern fast food, either falafel or shwarma in pita bread or hummus paste mopped up with pita, should cost no more than NIS 35 ($10). Otherwise there is the standard Western fast food fare: McDonald's burgers and fries (NIS 50; $14) or Domino's pizza (NIS 12 per slice; $3.50).

Jerusalem and Tel Aviv also have an especially wide selection of higher-end restaurants, ranging from French and Italian cuisine, through to Chinese and Japanese, with plenty of Middle Eastern options in between. Makhanei Yehuda market and the surrounding streets in Jerusalem, together with Carmel market in Tel Aviv and the nearby Kerem Hatamanim, have the biggest concentration of restaurants and eateries. Otherwise try downtown, Mamilla, or the German Colony in Jerusalem; or Jaffa port, Tel Aviv port, and most places in between in Tel Aviv.

It is worth making reservations, as the most popular restaurants can be booked more than a week ahead of time, especially on Thursday, Friday, and Saturday nights. While most Jerusalem restaurants are kosher, few in Tel Aviv are; Israeli restaurants are especially strong on vegetarian and vegan options.

Jerusalem

Abu Shukri
63 Al Wad Road (Via Dolorosa); tel: 02-627 1538; daily 8am–4.30pm, later in summer and on Sat; $

Arab restaurant in the Old City that is legendary for its hummus. Located in the Muslim quarter on the Via Dolorosa, this eatery, with its plain Arab working-class decor offers straightforward tasty, smooth hummus with various toppings, including tahini, fava beans, and pine nuts, as well as falafel, at very reasonable prices. Imitation is the best form of flattery and dozens of hummus restaurants have sprung up around Israel calling themselves Abu Shukri.

Agas Vetapuach
6 Safra Square; tel: 02-623 0280; Sun–Thu 11am–11pm; $$

Meaning pear and apple, this dairy restaurant serves excellent Italian fare in

Expect to pay the following for a three-course meal for one person
$ up to $25
$$ $26–50
$$$ $51–75
$$$$ over $75

a relaxed Jerusalem environment. The menu includes nine types of pasta with 14 sauces including classic Italian olive oil, garlic, tomato, and cream based sauces. Kosher.

Ahavat Hayam

11 Ben Tzvi Boulevard (in the Paz petrol station complex); tel: 02-623 6767; Sat–Thu noon–midnight; $$

Despite its unpromising location, this restaurant (the name of which translates to the love of the sea) serves up some of the city's best fish. Try the mullet or St Peter's fish (*tilapia*). All meals start out with garlic pita.

Al Dente

50 Ussishkin Street, Jerusalem; tel: 02-625 1479; Sun–Thu noon–11pm, Fri 11am–4pm, Sat 8pm–midnight; $$

Small neighborhood restaurant in Rehavia, offering its own unique and creative Italian cuisine at modest prices in an intimate and cosy atmosphere verging on cramped. There's the usual array of pastas and sauces, with some interesting fish dishes, including bream. Kosher non-meat menu.

Arabesque

American Colony Hotel, Nablus Road, Jerusalem; tel: 02-627 9777; daily 6.30am–midnight; $$$

Arabesque offers an à la carte menu with Middle Eastern gourmet dishes at their best as well as cordon bleu international cuisine in Jerusalem's landmark and oldest hotel.

Arcadia

10 Agrippas Street; tel: 02 624 0138; daily 7pm–10.30pm, Fri also 8am–4pm; $$$$

Tucked away in a tiny alleyway off Agrippas Street, this restaurant offers French and Mediterranean cuisine with Middle Eastern improvisations by its Iraqi-Jewish chef.

Aroma

Mamilla Pedestrian Mall; tel: 02-6241 304; Sun–Thu 8am–midnight, Fri 8am–4pm, Sat 8pm–midnight; $

This new branch of a national chain of quality coffee houses provides stirring views of the Old City walls with good value light meals and sandwiches. Kosher.

Azura

4 Haeshkol Street; tel: 02-6235 204; Sun–Thu 8.30am–4pm, Fri 8am–1 hour before sunset; $

A veteran Jerusalem restaurant, located in the Iraqi market section of Makhanei Yehuda market, Azura serves traditional North African dishes including hummus, *kubbe*, kebab, and rice.

Caffit

35 Emek Refaim; tel: 02-563 5284; Sun–Thu 7.30am–1am, Fri 7.30am–1 hour before sunset, Sat after sunset.

This is one of the city's best-known cafés in the fashionable German Col-

Crave Gourmet Street Food

ony, with good value salads and sandwiches. Caffit has spawned a chain of popular cafés throughout the city. Kosher.

Crave Gourmet Street Food

1 Hashikma Street; http://www.facebook.com/gotcrave; Sun–Thu noon–11.30pm, closes Fri before sunset, opens Sat after sunset; $$
Established by an American chef, this cramped eatery serves up US specialties, from hamburgers and corned beef sandwiches to tortillas. Kosher.

Darna

3 Horkenos Street; tel: 02-624 5406; Sun–Thu 7pm–11pm, Sat after sunset; $$$
Darna is a veteran restaurant offering North African food with a Berber influence and a Moroccan atmosphere, including authentic implements and ceremonial service. Try the phyllo-dough filled with Cornish hen. Kosher.

Dublin

4 Shammai Street; tel: 052-836 5323; daily 11am–3am; $
A piece of Ireland in Jerusalem, although late at night the emphasis is more on disco with plain Western food to go with the beer.

Eucalyptus

Felt alley, between 14 Hativat Yerushalayim and Dror Eliel Street; tel: 02-624 4331; www.the-eucalyptus.com; Sun–Thu 5pm–11pm; $$$

Eucalyptus offers an unusual choice of local foods, serving a contemporary interpretation of biblical cuisine beneath the Walls of the Old City Kosher.

Focaccia Bar Hamoshava

35 Emek Refaim, German Colony; tel: 02-538 7182; Sun–Thu 11am–midnight, Fri 8.30am–noon, Sat after sunset–midnight; $$
This restaurant serves good quality grilled meat and fish dishes in the heart of the German Colony, although – somewhat surprisingly – focaccia itself is not its forte. Kosher.

Fortuna

2 Haarmonim Street; tel: 02-500 1787; Sun–Thu noon–midnight, Fri noon–1 hour before sunset; $$
Good value steakhouse near the Makhanei Yehuda market, which takes pride in its fresh and well-seasoned meat. The restaurant serves up lots of appetizers to get your taste buds tingling. Kosher.

Hummus Ben Sira

3 Ben Sira Street; tel: 02-625 3893; Sun–Thu 11am–11pm, Fri 9am–4pm; $
Delicious hummus is served at this very reasonably priced eatery, which also has chicken dishes and is centrally located between downtown and the Mamilla Mall. Kosher.

La Regence

King David Hotel, 23 Ha Melekh David; tel:

Seafood dish at Alena

02-620 8795; Open Sun–Thu 7pm–10pm, Sat after sunset–midnight; $$$$
Located in the city's most prestigious hotel, this is considered the city's finest kosher restaurant, offering nouvelle cuisine and traditional French cooking, combining classical and innovative dishes. Kosher.

Link

3 Hama'alot Street; tel: 053-809 4510; daily noon–11pm; $$
This is an attractive bar and bistro in downtown Jerusalem with a diverse selection of foods and snacks set in an attractive old building and courtyard.

Mike's Place

37 Yafo Street, near Zion Square; tel: 02-267 0965; daily 11am–3am; $
English-style pub with live music and live TV soccer and a wide choice of draft beers and pub grub.

Notre Dame

8 Shivtei Yisra'el Street; tel: 02-628 8018; daily 7–11pm; $$$
Notre Dame is located in the magnificent hospice building of the same name opposite the Old City's New Gate. Owned by the Vatican, this is one of the city's finest restaurants and it offers surprisingly good value French fare.

Rimon Café

4 Lunz; tel: 02-625 2772; Sun–Thu 8am–midnight, Fri 8am–3pm, Sat after sunset–midnight; $$

The café/restaurant is a popular hangout at the bottom of the Ben Yehuda Street Mall with a choice of light meals and cakes. Kosher.

Simas

78 Agripas; tel: 02-423 3002; Sun–Thu noon–11pm, Fri noon–4pm, Sat after sunset–midnight; $$
Renowned for decades for its speedy service and good quality food, this is one of the city's city's best-value steak eateries. Try the Jerusalem mix meat dish. Kosher.

Tel Aviv

Abouelafia

4 Yefet Street, Yafo; tel: 03-682 8544; daily 11am–3am; $
This is Tel Aviv's best-known Middle Eastern fast food restaurant, by Jaffa's landmark clock tower – great for shwarma, falafel, and hummus.

Alena

Norman Hotel, 23–25 Nahmani Street; tel: 03-543 5400; Mon–Sat 7am–11am and daily 12.30–3pm and 6–10.30pm; $$$$
This restaurant, located in the city's most exclusive hotel, serves European and Mediterranean favorites with traditional Japanese cuisine thrown in for good measure – delicious, but extremely expensive.

Benny Hadayag

Tel Aviv port; tel: 053-944 4154; daily noon–midnight; $$

Shakshuka in Tel Aviv

Benny Hadayag is one of Israel's leading fish restaurants, where you can also savor the atmosphere of Tel Aviv's re-invention of its Old Port as a leisure complex.

Café Noir
43 Ahad Ha'Am Street; www.en.cafenoir. co.il; 03-566 3018; Sun–Thu noon–11.30pm Fri, Sat noon–midnight; $$$
Not a café as the name suggests but an upscale brasserie in an elegant setting in an old Tel Aviv building with a Viennese flavor and Mediterranean twist. Try the schnitzel.

Café Nordau
51 Nordau Boulevard; tel: 052-423 9383; Sat–Thu 11am–1am, Fri 11am–6pm; $
This trendy sidewalk café for snacks is popular with the city's LGBTQ community and in addition to the good food is a great place to meet people.

Chinese Wall
26 Mikve Israel; tel: 03-560 3974; Sun–Thu 12–11pm, Fri 12–4pm, Sat after sunset–11pm; $$
This Chinese restaurant is one of the city's few top-quality kosher restaurants, outside of the hotels. If you start out with the piping hot dumplings and wonton soup, you won't have much room left for the main courses.

Erez Yemenite Restaurant
28 Nakhliel Street, Kerem Hatemanim; tel: 052-255 3808; Sun–Thu 10am–8pm, Fri 10am–4pm, closed Sat; $

This is a traditional family restaurant in the heart of the city's Yemenite quarter (Kerem Hatemanim). Start off with the classic Yemenite soup and pita, then house specialties include meatball and okra in tomato sauce and a range of grilled meat and fish dishes.

Lev Harachav (Wide Heart)
10 Rabbi Akiva Street, Carmel Market; tel 054-473 6622; Sun–Fri noon–1.30pm; $
A no-nonsense, tasty and inexpensive authentic Israeli restaurant, with excellent hummus. Kosher.

Meat Kitchen
65 Yigal Alon Street; tel 03-536 4755; Sun–Wed noon–midnight, Thu noon–1am, Fri noon–5pm, Sat after sunset–midnight; $$$
A chef restaurant for meat lovers, with artistically presented dishes. Kosher.

Meshek Barzilay
6 Ahad Ha'am Street, Neve Tzedek; tel: 03-516 6329; www.meshekbarzilay.co.il/en/; Sun 8am–4pm Mon–Thu 8am–11pm Sat 9am–11pm; $$
One of Tel Aviv's longest-established vegan restaurants, Meshek Barzilay is a fine example of the creativity developed by the city's vegan chefs. Even the most committed carnivores adore dishes like pumpkin steak, cashew and walnut pizzas, and mushroom and lentil burgers.

Molly Bloom's Traditional Irish Pub
2 Mendele Street; tel: 03-522 1558; Sun–Thu 4pm–2am, Fri 2pm–2am, Sat

Diners on Rothschild Boulevard

3pm–2am; $$

The name says it all. Molly Bloom's is one of many Irish pubs near the seafront with an authentic atmosphere, live Irish music, sport on TV; expensive beer and pub grub.

Orna and Ella

33 Sheinkin Street; tel: 03-525 2085; daily 10am–midnight; $$

On trendy Sheinkin Street, this started as a café and developed into a bistro with an emphasis on homemade breads, pastries, and pastas.

Rahmo Hagadol

98 Derekh Menachem Begin; tel: 03-562 1022; Sun–Thu 9am–5pm Fri 9am–2pm; $

This is the pick of Tel Aviv's veteran hummus and falafel eateries, which has remarkably kept going even though it is located very near the upscale Sarona complex. Rahmo Hagadol is excellent, tasty, clean and astonishingly cheap. Kosher.

Saluf & Sons

80 Nahlat Binyamin Street; tel: 03-522 1344; Sun–Thu 11am–11pm, Fri 10am–6pm; $

This Yemenite hummus and meat restaurant has retained its modest atmosphere and low prices, despite its popularity with the trendy Tel Aviv society. Try the Yemenite specialties, including *kubaneh* yeast bread and the flaky *malawakh* pancake wrap. Meat eaters will like the beef stew with couscous

Shakshukia

94 Ben Yehuda Street; tel: 03-522 3433; Sun–Thu noon–4pm, 6.30–10.30pm, Fri 11am–4pm; $$

This restaurant, as the name implies, focuses on shakshuka, a popular local dish of eggs poached in a sauce of tomatoes, chilli peppers, and onions, and spiced with cumin, paprika, and cayenne pepper. Meat dishes are also served, including turkey shwarma shakshuka. The restaurant has vegan and gluten free options.

The Old Man and the Sea

101 Retzif Ha'alyah Hashnia, Jaffa; tel: 03-544 8820; 11am–midnight; $$

Middle Eastern restaurant on Jaffa port dockside serves an excellent mezze salad spread followed by grilled meats and fish. The waiters put on an impressive show, collecting up all the plates in one go, however large the number of diners.

Topolompopo

14 Hasolelim Street; tel: 03-691 0691; Sun–Thu noon–11pm, Fri 6pm–11pm; $$$$

Asian fusion food in what is considered one of the finest and most expensive restaurants in the city.

Vong

15 Rothschild Boulevard; tel: 03-633 7171; daily noon–midnight; www.vong.co.il; $$

Israel's premier Vietnamese restaurant offers tasty cuisine and reasonable

Doniana in Akko

prices for one of Tel Aviv's most expensive addresses. Vong is famous for its delicious steamed buns and range of vegan options.

TYO

17 Montefiore Street; tel: 03-930 0333; www.tyo.co.il/en; daily 7pm–midnight; $$$

TYO is perhaps Tel Aviv's finest Japanese restaurant specializing in seafood, and is located in a lounge-bar environment in an elegant and striking old building. The restaurant has a reputation for serving up some of the city's finest sushi.

416

16 Ha'arba'ah Street; tel: 03-775 5060; www.416.co.il; daily noon–11pm; $$

This is a New York-style vegan restaurant with high quality, creative meat substitutes.

Akko

Doniana

Salah Al-Batzri Street, Pizani Harbour, next to the lighthouse; tel: 04-991 0001; daily noon–11pm; $$

Overlooking the Mediterranean near ancient Akko port, the pick of the city's restaurants specializes in fish and seafood as well as a wide variety of salads and dips.

Caesarea

Limani Bistro

Caesarea Port; tel: (04) 610 0022; daily noon–11pm; $$

Limani is a fish restaurant in a delightful location overlooking the old Crusader port, with the usual selection of delicious Eastern Mediterranean fish and salads.

Galilee

Dag Al Hadan

Tel Dan, near Kiryat Shmona; tel: 04-695 0225; daily noon–10pm; $

No visit to the Galilee is complete without a meal at Dag Al Hadan, where fresh fish pulled out of the River Jordan is served in a tranquil rural atmosphere. The house specialty is trout.

Decks Restaurant

13 Gdud Barak Street, Tiberias; tel: 04-671 0800; daily noon–11pm; $$

Decks provides a stirring opportunity to eat the biblical St Peter's fish (*tilapia*) while overlooking the Sea of Galilee. The restaurant also serves excellent steaks and has vegetarian dishes.

Little Tiberias Restaurant

5 Kishon Street, Tiberias; tel 04-679 2148; noon–midnight; $$

This is a good value steakhouse and seafood restaurant with vegetarian and vegan options.

Haifa

Dan Panorama Haifa Restaurant

107 Hanassi Avenue, Central Carmel; tel: 04-835 2222; daily 7am–noon, 6pm–11pm; $$$

Shawarma

This hotel restaurant serves delicious buffet-style Israeli breakfasts and meat/fish dinners with the best view of Haifa Bay from Mount Carmel. Kosher.

Douzan

35 Ben Gurion Street, German Colony; tel: 054-944 3301; daily 11am–midnight; $$

Douzan is renowned for an unusual fusion of oriental and western food in an eastern ambience in the delightful German Colony. The Arab-owned restaurant's diverse cuisine echoes the relative ethnic and religious tolerance of the city.

Fattoush

38 Ben Gurion Street, Germany Colony; tel: 04-852 4930; daily 11am–midnight; $$

This is another excellent Arab-owned restaurant in the German Colony, beneath the Bahá'í Hillside Gardens, with a diverse array of creative Middle Eastern dishes for vegetarians and meat-eaters.

La Terrazza

46 Moriah Boulevard; tel: 04-810 1100; Sun–Thu noon–midnight, Fri–Sat 8pm–1am; $$

La Terrazza serves good value Italian and Mediterranean cuisine with a great view from the terrace.

Shawarma Ahim Sabah

37 Allenby; tel: 04-855 2188; daily 11am–midnight; $

Located in midtown Hadar, this Middle Eastern eatery specializes in meat cut from the spit and eaten in pitta with a wide range of salads and relishes.

Yan Yan

28 Yafo, Haifa Port; tel: 04-866 0022; Sat–Thu 11am–11pm, Fri 11am–midnight; $$

Yan Yan serves excellent tasting and good-value Vietnamese and Chinese cuisine in the downtown port area.

Nazareth

Tishreen

56 El-Bishara Street, Near Mary's Well; tel: 04-608 4666; daily 11am–11pm; $$

This restaurant near the Church of the Annunciation offers traditional Middle East and Mediterranean fare. Specialty dishes include Arab pizza topped with chicken and aubergine stuffed with pesto.

O'Connell's Bar

NIGHTLIFE

Nightlife starts late in Israel and is very vibrant. From 11pm onward, Israelis are out on the streets of Jerusalem, Tel Aviv, and virtually every Israeli city. Street-side cafés and restaurants are busy until well after midnight, while bars and discos have a brisk trade right through the night. Because Friday and Saturday constitute the weekend, Thursday night is a big night out.

Tel Aviv seafront and other hotspots are crowded right through the night. Bohemian Florentin is another popular nightspot in Tel Aviv as well as Yafo near the flea market, Tel Aviv port and Old Yafo port. Rock, jazz, folk and pop music are the usual fare for live music. The focus of nightlife in Jerusalem is the Makhanei Yehuda market and surrounding streets, as well as the Russian Compound and eastern end of Jaffa Road and the Talpiot industrial zone.

Jerusalem

Cinema City
10 Yitzhak Rabin Boulevard; tel 02-752 6700; Sun–Thu 11am–3am, Fri 1pm– sunset, Sat sunset–3am.

This 15-screen multiplex theater, within a large mall with stores, cafés, restaurants, and bars, gets very busy at night.

Mike's Place
Courtyard off 39 Yafa (Jaffa) Road also accessible from Yoel Salomon Street; tel: 052-267 0753; Sun–Thu 11am–3am, Fri 11am–sunset, Sat: after sunset.

This is one of Jerusalem's most popular pubs in the heart of the city's downtown, with a labyrinth of different bars and outside seating. Plenty of pub grub, live music most nights, and Mike's Place is also very popular for live TV sport broadcasts, including English Premier League soccer games.

O'Connell's Bar
63 Ets Khayim, Makhanei Yehuda; tel: 02-623 2232; Sun–Thu 1pm–3am, Fri: 11am– sunset, Sat sunset–3am

This is one of just dozens of small bars and eateries in the Makhnei Yehuda market, which buzzes with loud music until the early hours of the morning. Just sit down, order some draft beer, and watch the people go – and often dance – by. The high-energy of Jerusalem's night revelers is quite remarkable.

Yellow Submarine
13 Harekhavim Street, Talpiot; tel: 02-679 4040; Sat–Thu 10pm–1am

The Yellow Submarine bills itself as Jerusalem's premiere live-music concert venue, but this is really more like a very big pub with local talent, from jazz, rock, folk, and blues to cover bands

Crowd at Hangar 11

appearing almost every night along with stand-up comedy and poetry readings. There is an admission charge of $10–15.

Tel Aviv

Hangar 11

Tel Aviv port; tel: 03-602 0888; daily 7pm–midnight

One of Tel Aviv's premier concert venues, located in what was, until 1990, a warehouse. Live music performances and cultural events most nights at the northern end of the bustling Tel Aviv port on the seafront. Admission charge.

Haoman 17

88 Abarbanel Street; tel 03-681 3636; daily 7pm–2am

Located in the hipster Florentin quarter, Haoman 17 is one of Israel's best-known nightclubs, with live music and dance performances, that is also particularly popular with the LGBTQ community. Admission charge.

Levontin 7

7 Levontin Street; tel: 03-560 5084; daily 6pm–midnight.

This is one of Tel Aviv's best known nightclubs, with live performances every night of almost every type of music imaginable as well as local stand-up comics and other cultural events. The club has several bars and a vegan pizza restaurant. Admission charge.

Teder.FM

9 Derekh Jaffa; tel 03-571 9622; daily 7pm–3am

Teder.FM bills itself as Tel Aviv's hipster capital, offering drink, food, live bands, and and DJs. The place has a great atmosphere, with both indoor and outdoor bars and restaurants.

Tel Aviv Center for the Performing Arts

19 Shaul Hamelekh Boulevard; tel: 03-692 7777; Sun–Fri 7pm–midnight, closed Sat

This very impressive art complex houses nightly cultural performances and is home to the Israel Opera and Carmeri theater company. Live music, ballet, art and photo exhibitions, and a café and bar are also on offer.

The Block

157 Shalma Road; tel: 03-537 8002; daily 6pm–3am

The Block is the place to go late – that is to say early in the morning. This dance club and large bar only really gets rocking after about 1am. The line-up includes DJs and live bands. Admission charge.

Jerusalem Light Rail

A–Z

A

Age Restrictions

Alcohol is served only to those 18 and over and drink-drive laws are strictly enforced, with drivers of 23 or under not allowed to have any alcohol whatsoever in their bloodstream. The age of consent is 16 in Israel regardless of sexual orientation. In certain instances, the age of consent is 14, providing the partner is not more than three years older.

B

Budgeting

Israel is one of the world's most expensive countries and Jerusalem and Tel Aviv are Israel's most expensive cities. Even so it is possible to live cheaply: public transportation is inexpensive, as are youth hostels and falafel and hummus eateries.

Food and Drink

A third of a litre (a little over half a pint) of beer, or a glass of house wine is likely to cost $7–9; a small bottle of mineral water, $2 although it's the same price for a large bottle in a supermarket; McDonald's hamburger and fries about $15; three-course meal in a city center restaurant with a drink and tip around $40; the best value food is falafel or shwarma (gyro) in pita with as much

salad as you want for $10 or a plate of hummus and pita for $8.

Hotel Prices

Accommodations are expensive and you will be hard-pressed to find anything for less than $80 per night, except for the most basic youth hostel or very cheap hotel. A more comfortable hotel is going to be around $140 per night. It is advisable reserve flights and accommodations before coming to Israel.

Transport Costs

A flat-fare bus ticket in a city costs under $2, and the bus or train between Tel Aviv and Jerusalem around $6. Long-distance buses and trains include a free intra-city bus ride if you have the Rav-Kav multi-ride card. A taxi between the two cities would cost $40.

Admission Charges

The major museums are relatively inexpensive, charging an entrance fee of about $10, with half-price entry for children and seniors, and reductions available for students. The Israel Museum charges half-price for repeat visits; the Yad Vashem Holocaust Museum is free. The Israel National Parks Authority, which runs the major archeological sites, charges $6 admission fee, again with half-price entry for children and seniors. It could be worth buying a ticket

Cranes at Hula Valley National Park

for the entire country's national parks for $25; tel: 02-500 6261, or 3639 from within Israel. Most beaches are free.

C

Children

Israelis love children, who are expected to be seen and heard, and people should not feel threatened by the forward behavior of strangers in the street or at the next restaurant table toward their children. They are likely to engage in conversation with your child and offer all types of candies.

Eating: Restaurants, hotels, and cafés are very flexible in meeting children's fussy food needs, but tend not to have a formal children's menu. McDonald's, Burger King, and Pizza Hut are always near at hand for kids who like familiar fast food.

Accommodations: Many hotels operate baby sitting services and are flexible in adding beds in the parents' room for a minimal rate. Here, too, good negotiating skills and persistence can help.

Transportation: Children under 5 travel for free on buses, but thereafter pay full fare unless a multiride ticket is acquired. On trains children under 5 go free; children between the ages of 5 and 10 get a 20 percent discount. Children under 4 must be harnessed into special seats when traveling in cars, but not in taxis.

Clothing

Dress in Israel is informal. Few people wear jackets and ties in the summer, except for business occasions. The hot weather makes it tempting to wear less rather than more, but even in the summer Jerusalem can get cool in the evenings. Be sure to bring some conservative clothes for visiting religious sites though. It is recommended to keep arms, legs, and shoulders covered to prevent sunburn. Also, wear a hat for sun protection.

Crime and Safety

Israel has a high rate of non-violent crimes (theft from homes, cars, other property, and pick-pocketing) but relatively little violent crime. Do not leave valuables in hotel rooms or cars, or leave wallets sticking out of pockets. In terms of violent crime, the security situation is the most pressing problem, but incidents are few and far between. Do not leave unattended baggage in a public place – the police may blow it up. Report all suspicious packages. Before visiting the West Bank or Gaza ask about the prevailing security situation. Police, tel: 100 (emergencies); 110 (information). Marijuana/cannabis is illegal, but prosecutions are rarely brought. However, tourists should act with extreme caution.

Customs

Tourists with nothing to declare may choose the Green Channel. Tourists bringing in very expensive equipment (for example large cameras), even if exempt from duty, must use the Red Channel.

Every adult tourist may bring into the country, without payment of duty: *eau*

Nakhalat Binyamin, Tel Aviv

de Cologne or perfume not exceeding 0.2 liters (0.44 pint); wine up to 2 liters and other alcoholic drinks not exceeding 1 liter; tobacco or cigars not exceeding 250 grams or 250 cigarettes; gifts up to $200, including food not exceeding 3kg (6.5lb), on condition that no single type of food exceeds 1kg (2.2lb).

Portable, expensive electronic items such as cameras, video cameras, and laptop computers may be taken into the country duty-free if they are taken out on departure. Two laptops are allowed if one is for personal use, and one for professional use. Few checks are made these days on compact, inconspicuous items.

The customs authorities are entitled to demand deposits on any article brought in by a tourist or sent separately. This is enforced only for very expensive professional equipment. Deposits are returned when leaving Israel with the article.

D

Disabled Travelers

For a list of tourist services for travelers with mobility issues contact Yad Sarah (Yad Sarah House, Kiryat Weinberg, 124 Herzl Boulevard, Jerusalem 96187; tel: 02-644 4444; http://yadsarah.org.uk). This website lists those museums and other places that are accessible for those in wheelchairs.

In theory, much of Israel, including public transportation, is highly accessible for those in wheelchairs, but in practice cars parked on sidewalks and cramped city centers can make life difficult.

E

Electricity

Standard voltage in Israel is 220 volts AC (single phase 50 cycles). Most plugs are three-pin, but in some instances can be two-pin. Adaptors and transformers can be purchased throughout Israel.

Embassies & Consulates

Jerusalem
UK Consulate
Bet Ha'Omot Building, 101 Hebron Road, 1st Floor, West Jerusalem.
Tel: 02-671 7724.
US Embassy & Consulate General
14 David Flusser Street
Tel: 02-630 4000

Tel Aviv
Australian Embassy
23 Yehuda Halevy Street
Tel: 03-695 5000
www.australianembassy.org.il
Canadian Embassy
3 Nirim Street, 63405
Tel: 03-636 3300
Visa section, 7 Khavakuk ha-Navi
Tel: 03-544 2878
www.dfaitmaeic.gc.ca/telaviv
Embassy of the Republic of South Africa
12 Abba Hillel Street, Ramat Gan
Tel: 03-525 2566

Me'a She'arim, Jerusalem

Ireland
2 Jabotinsky Street, Ramat Gan
Tel: 03-696 4166
UK Embassy
Tel: 03-725 1222
Consular Section, 1 Ben Yehuda
US Embassy Branch Office
71 Ha-Yarkon
Tel: 03-519 7575

Emergencies

In case of a serious accident or emergency, telephone for an ambulance 101 and/or police 100. The Fire Service is 102, and 103 is the emergency number for the electricity company.

Etiquette

Israelis are informal, direct, and brusque but also warm and welcoming and especially respectful to the elderly. In Jewish religious neighborhoods and Arab towns, immodest dress is inadvisable.

H

Health

Israel has advanced healthcare services with all citizens guaranteed medical attention by law.

Vaccinations: There are no vaccination requirements for tourists entering Israel, except those who are arriving from infected areas.

Health Insurance: Visitors are advised to have medical insurance as hospital costs are expensive. Lists of doctors, dentists, and on-duty pharma-

cies are available from hotel receptions or online. Seeing a doctor is likely to cost at least $40. For more serious situations, go to a hospital emergency room (choodor miyun). Sunburn, sunstroke, and dehydration can be avoided by drinking large amounts of water and staying out of the sun. Tap water is as drinkable as anywhere in the developed world; mineral waters is available everywhere.

Most pharmacies are open 9am–9pm and have English-speaking staff. Some pharmacies stay open on a 24-hour rotation basis. Consult local media to find out which pharmacy is open through the night.

Phone **101** for an ambulance.

Hours and Holidays

Most places are generally open all day Sunday–Thursday, and close Friday lunchtime until Saturday night. Stores are open long hours, usually 9am–9pm Sunday–Thursday, but close at 2pm on Friday and are closed Saturday. Banks are open Sunday–Thursday 8.30am–1pm. Some branches stay open until 3pm and some are open in the late afternoon, 4–6pm on Monday and Thursday. Some branches open Friday morning, all banks are closed on Saturday and some are closed Sunday. Places of entertainment are open until late. Bars are usually open until 3am.

The following Jewish festivals are also public holidays:
March/April: first and last days of Passover (Pesach).
May/June: Independence Day, Shavuot.

Letterbox in Jaffa

Sept/Oct: Jewish New Year (Rosh Hashanah); Yom Kippur, first and last days of Succot.

The eve of a festival is like Friday, with most businesses, banks, post offices, etc. closing at lunch time.

I

Internet

With its high-tech culture, Israel places major emphasis on Wi-fi and internet access. Not only do virtually all hotels, restaurants, bars, and stores offer free Wi-fi, but many public places in Tel Aviv and Jerusalem also have free Wi-fi too, including Tel Aviv's seafront and beaches. Most Israeli city centers also have reasonably priced Internet cafés; being a small densely populated country there is cellphone coverage with data virtually everywhere.

L

Language

Israelis have very strong English language skills and enjoy practicing their English on tourists.

LGBTQ Travelers

Israel in general and Tel Aviv in particular are very tolerant of the LGBTQ community. Most cities, including Jerusalem, have an annual pride parade and LGBTQ clubs that fly the rainbow flag. Nevertheless, gay and lesbian travelers would be advised to keep a lower profile in religious Jewish neighborhoods and Arab locations.

M

Mail

Israel's government-owned postal authority charges around $2 for letters and postcards sent abroad. Mail has become very slow in recent years and can take several weeks even for a domestic letter to arrive. Express and super-express are available, taking only a few days for much higher fees, depending on weight and destination. DHL, Fed-Ex, and other international shipping services also operate. Stamps can be bought in post offices and in souvenir stores selling postcards.

Major post offices are open all day while smaller branches have variable hours. Post offices usually have a machine at the entrance dispensing numbers, so that you do not have to wait in a line. Waiting time can be long, but it is also possible to make an appointment online at www.israelpost.co.il. However, the service is only available in Hebrew. On Friday afternoon, Saturday, and holidays post offices close all day. Other services at post offices include paying bills and traffic and parking fines, sending currency through Western Union, and currency exchange.

Jerusalem Main Post Office: 217 Jaffa Road, Sun–Thu 8am–5pm

Tel Aviv: 61 Hayarkon Street, Sun–Thu 8am–6pm, Fri 8am–midday

Bauhaus architecture, Tel Aviv

Media

Israel has a wide range of English language media options and the country also enjoys broad coverage in the international media.

Newspapers and News Websites

Israel's has two daily newspapers in English – the right-wing *Jerusalem Post* and the left-wing *Haaretz*, which is published in conjunction with the *International Herald Tribune*. Both are published six days a week with no newspaper on Saturday. The Friday (weekend) edition of the *Jerusalem Post* has an English-language listing of what's going on in the arts, music, theater, television, and radio. It also carries useful information about medical services, religious services, etc.

Both papers have websites www.jpost.com and www.haaretz.com (paywall). There are also many Israeli news websites in English including the *Times of Israel* www.timesofisrael.com and *Globes* (finance and business) https://en/globes.co.il/en

Radio and Television

Israel's cable and digital TV stations offer a range of international news broadcasts in English including *Sky, Fox, BBC,* and *CNN. Channel i24* offers English-language news. International stations such as the *BBC World Service* are also available in Israel.

Money

Currency

Israel's currency is the New Israeli Shekel (NIS), less commonly known as ISL, and is divided into 100 agorot. Bills are issued in four denominations: 20 NIS (red), 50 NIS (green), 100 NIS (yellow), and 200 NIS (blue). Change comes in the bronze coins of 10 agorot, half a shekel; and silver coins of 1 shekel, 2 shekels, 5 shekels and 10 shekels (silver and gold).

Credit Cards

Credit cards are accepted everywhere.

In the event of losing your card:

VISA, tel: (03) 617 8800.
Mastercard/ Eurocard and Diners Club, tel: (03) 572 3666.
American Express, Tel. 1-800-877-877.

ATMs

ATMs are everywhere, although charges are lower at those in the walls of banks rather than stand-alone machines in stores and malls. Many ATMs in Jerusalem and Tel Aviv will also issue US dollars and euros as well as shekels.

Changing Money

Banks and Bureaux de Change are everywhere and it is usually much more convenient in terms of time to change money or cash travelers' checks at a Bureau de Change. The NIS is stable and floats freely against the world's major currencies, with a revised exchange rate each day.

Inside the Church of the Holy Sepulchre, Jerusalem

Tipping

In restaurants and cafés, a service charge is rarely included; a 10–15 percent tip is expected. Most places will allow the tip to be paid for by credit card, added to the main check. Israelis do not tip taxi drivers, but drivers will often try to manipulate tourists into tipping. Hotel staff such as porters should be tipped and hairdressers also expect a small tip.

Taxes

17-percent value added tax (VAT) is charged on all items (except in Eilat) and should be included in prices displayed. Tourists paying hotel and car rental bills in foreign currency are exempt from VAT. VAT on purchases of more than $50 can be claimed back at Ben Gurion International Airport on presentation of a tax receipt. Under anti-money-laundering laws, sums over NIS 50,000 brought into the country must be declared.

R

Religion

Israel is officially a Jewish State, although Orthodox Jewry is fragmented among many different sects and communities. There are a small number of Conservative and Reform Jewish communities. Most Arabs are Sunni Muslim and there is a small Christian minority, split between Orthodox churches and Catholics, and some members of the Bahá'í Faith too. Most Israelis are actually secular and the atmosphere is very

tolerant although occasionally local religious tensions can spill over, but this will not affect tourists.

Restrooms

Israeli toilets are of the standard Western variety, with public facilities usually available in popular tourist locations. If not, people are usually tolerant about use of restrooms in restaurants, cafés, bars, hotels, and even banks.

S

Smoking

By law Israelis are not supposed to smoke in public places and certainly not in shopping malls, restaurants, cafés, bars, and museums. Hotels usually offer smoking and non-smoking rooms. However, the law is ignored by some communities and observed by others. Visitors would be wise to refrain from smoking in public.

T

Telephones

Israel's country code is 972 when phoning from abroad and it is 970 for the Palestinian territories. There are few public phones remaining in Israel.

Landline Area Codes in Israel

02 Jerusalem
03 Tel Aviv
04 Northern Israel
08 Southern Israel
09 Herzliya and Netanya

Minaret of Jaffa's Jama El-Baher Mosque, and the Mediterranean Sea

Overseas Calls
Some country codes:
1 US and Canada
44 UK
61 Australia
64 New Zealand
353 Ireland
27 South Africa

Cellphone Operators
Israel has good quality and cheap cellphone networks, which work on the main North American and European bands. Tariffs are low and some plans include free overseas calls to landlines. Local SIM cards can be purchased from many outlets for about $20 and local smartphones can be rented for about $10 per day.

Useful Numbers
Call **144** for directory enquiries
100 Police Emergency
110 Police Information
101 Ambulance
102 Fire Brigade

Time Zone
Israel is at Coordinated Universal Time (UTC). UTC does not observe daylight saving, so Israel is 2 hours ahead of of GMT in winter, and 1 hour in summer; 7 hours ahead of New York in winter, and 6 in summer. Summer time lasts in line with Europe from the end of March to the end of October.

Tourist Information
There are helpful tourist information offices in London, New York, and all Israel's major cities.
https://info.goisrael.com/en/ (official site of Israel's Ministry of Tourism)

Canada
Tel: 1-416 964 3784
E-mail: JerryA@goisrael.gov.il

UK
London W1A 8GP
Tel: (20) 7299 1111
E-mail: sharone@goisrael.gov.il

US
New York
Tel: 1 212 499 5655
E-mail: info-ny@goisrael.gov.il
Chicago
Tel: 1-312 803 7080
JillD@goisrael.gov.il
Los Angeles
Tel: 1-323 658 7463
E-Mail: anatb@goisrael.com
Atlanta
Tel: 1-404 541-2770
E-mail: Director-Atlanta@goisrael.gov.il

Israel
Ben Gurion Airport Tourist Information
Arrivals Hall. Open daily, 24 hours
Tel: 03-975 4256
Jerusalem Jaffa Gate
Tel: 02-627 1422
Sat–Thu 8.30am–5pm, Fri 8.30am–1.30pm

Ferry in Haifa

Tel Aviv, Municipal Building
Ibn Gbriol.
Tel: 03-521 8500.
46 Herbert Samuel Street
Tel: 03-516 6188
Tel Aviv offices open Sun–Thu 9.30am–
5.30pm, Fri 9am–noon. Closed Saturday

Tours and Guides

So much history gets missed without an expert guide to explain the significance of each site, so it is well worth joining an organized tour. Major tour bus companies include:

Egged Tours
Tel: 03-920 3992 www.eggedtours.com
United Tours
Tel: 03-617 3333 www.unitedtours.co.il/english.asp
Tal Limousine VIP Services
Tel: 03-975 4044 www.tal-limousine.com

Transportation

Arrival

Few visitors to Israel arrive by land, however there are land crossings from Egypt at Taba (near Eilat) and from Jordan (near Eilat, the Allenby Bridge and near Beit Shean). Some cruise ships call in at Haifa and Ashdod ports.

Airport

Ben Gurion International Airport is the main hub for international air traffic. It is 15km (9 miles) from Tel Aviv, and 50km (30 miles) from Jerusalem. There are two terminals: Terminal 3 for international passengers; and Terminal 1 for domestic flights and international passengers on low-cost airlines. There is a free shuttle bus service between Terminals 3 and 1 and the parking lots.

The airport has ATMs, banks, and a post office, which is open 24 hours a day (except Friday night/Saturday).

Ben Gurion International Airport information, including arrivals and departure times, 03-975 5555. Airport Government Tourist Office: 03-975 4256.

To and from the Airport: There is a rail link from Terminal 3 to Jerusalem and Tel Aviv.

Taxis: Taxis to Jerusalem cost about $50–60 and to Tel Aviv about $30–35.

Shared Taxis: Cost about $20 per person from Jerusalem to Tel Aviv. To book a shared taxi from your hotel or any other address in Jerusalem back to the airport, phone Nesher: 02-625 7227; or 1-599 500 205.

Sde Dov Airport, Tel Aviv's city airport has mainly domestic flights and some international flights to Greece and Cyprus.

Public Transportation

RavKav Smart Card – Tourists planning to spend much of their visit traveling on public transportation are advised to purchase a RavKav smart card multi-travel ticket which can be used interchangeably on buses, trains, the Jerusalem Light Rail and Haifa Carmelit. The tickets can be purchased online https://www.rail.co.il/en/pages/ravkavform.aspx or upon presentation of a passport at bus stations, train sta-

A Tel Aviv bus

tions and other service points, including the airport station. The cards provide discounts including free intra-city extension trips after an inter-city trip, and multiride inter-city trips within a two-hour period.

Buses are the most common means of public transportation.

Egged information: tel: 03-694 8888. Route details and timetables are available in English at www.egged.co.il. The site offers updated information about discounted and multiride tickets for various periods and in various cities, discounts for children and students, bus maps, etc. Egged runs the urban routes in Jerusalem.

Egged Lost Property: *2800
Dan Lost Property *3456

Dan Bus: Information on city buses in the Greater Tel Aviv region, tel: 03-639 4444; www.dan.co.il/english/

Times: Buses do not run from Friday before sundown until Saturday after sundown. Inter-urban bus services start around 6am and finish in the early evening except for the Tel Aviv–Jerusalem and Tel Aviv–Haifa lines which continue until midnight. Urban services run from 5am to just after midnight.

Locations: The Jerusalem Central Bus Station is at the western entrance to the city. The Tel Aviv Central Bus Station is a vast shopping mall complex on Levinski in the south of the city (connected to Haganah train station) although there is also a large bus station in Arlozorov Street by Tel Aviv Savidor Central Station.

Trains: Tickets are more expensive than for comparable bus rides. There is a station at Ben Gurion Airport with a fast-link to Jerusalem and Tel Aviv. For information, tel: (03) 577 4000, www.rail.co.il.

Lost property *5700

There is a map of the Israel Railway network at https://www.rail.co.il/en/pages/stationsnlines.aspx

There are no train services on the Sabbath, or on Jewish holidays.

Jerusalem Light Rail: A tram system operating from northern Jerusalem via the Old City's Damascus Gate, the city center along Jaffa Road to the train/central bus station to Herzl Boulevard and Yad Vashem. Flat fare tickets can be bought on-line at www.citypass.co.il or at automatic ticket machines at each stop, and RavKav cards can be used.

Tel Aviv Light Rail: This service is under construction. The first line – the Red Line – is scheduled to open in 2021.

Shared Taxis (*Sherut*): These operate in and between main cities including on Shabbat. Individuals share a mini-bus, which can take up to 10 people at a fixed price, usually equivalent to the bus fare for the same route. In Jerusalem *sheruts* between cities leave from near the central bus station, and from the city center including on Shabbat. In Tel Aviv the *sheruts* leave from near the Central Bus Station for most cities. Local *sheruts* in Tel Aviv follow the main bus routes, making similar stops in quicker time and charging the same fare.

Sarona Market, Tel Aviv

Taxis: Taxis offer a quick and convenient mode of travel in Israel. You can phone for a taxi in any major city, or hail one in the street, or use Uber or Gett apps. All taxis have meters, and their operation is compulsory. Tipping is not compulsory, but is appreciated. Prices are fixed between cities, and the driver will tell you your fare in advance, or show you the official price list if you ask for it.

Driving

Israelis drive on the right with much horn-honking, overtaking on the inside, and weaving in and out traffic. With well over 3.5 million vehicles on the roads, Israel has one of the world's most densely populated road systems. There are around 350 fatalities each year from road accidents, a rate comparable with death rates on Western European roads.

Laws are strictly enforced. Seat belts must be worn at all times (front and back) and children under four strapped into appropriate seats. Speed limits are 90–120kmh (56–75mph) on highways and 50–70kmh (31–43mph) in urban areas. There are many speed and traffic light cameras on highways, with fines of up to $250 for exceeding the speed limit by more than 10 percent or driving through a red light.

Using a phone not in a hands-free installation is an offense, which police penalize with a $250 fine. Drinking and driving laws are strictly enforced.

Israelis tend to move off very quickly at traffic lights the second they turn green, making it especially dangerous to jump a red light, even before the one-second grace that the police give drivers before issuing a ticket.

Fuel is about the same price as Western Europe. In Eilat, a VAT-free zone, you do not pay the 17 percent VAT charge on fuel.

Parking is difficult in city centers and it is best to look for a parking lot. If a curb is marked blue and white, you can pay by downloading an app – good for the entire country. – **Pango** www.pango.co.il or **Cellopark** www.cellopark.co.il If you fail to pay you are liable for a $30 fine. Do not ignore red and white marked curbs or No Parking signs. If you park here you may be clamped or even towed away.

Toll roads

Highway 6: The toll is collected electronically and car rental companies charge a handling fee for using Highway Six.

Tel Aviv Fast Lane: The toll is from $2 up to $30 depending on how badly jammed the highway is, and there is an extra handling fee for vehicles not registered in advance. The toll is clearly marked at the entrance to the lane. Vehicles with four passengers including the driver travel free but you must register with an inspector half way along. It is also possible to pay the toll to the inspector and avoid handling fees, especially with a rented car. There is also a free park-and-ride service in the lane with buses to Tel Aviv's Azrieli Center and Ramat Gan's Diamond Exchange.

Mary Magdalene's Tomb, Jerusalem

Car Rental

Car rental companies require drivers to be over 21 and to have held a full license for at least one year. Drivers must present an international driving license, or national license if written in English or French, plus a passport, and and international credit card.

Many of the world's principal car rental companies have outlets with branches at the airports and around the major cities. Israel's largest car-rental company, Eldan, also has offices overseas.

Car rental costs around $250 a week for a small saloon or $350 a week for a medium-sized car. Note that car rental companies will deduct any parking and police fines, and tolls, from your credit card, plus a handling fee. Payments in foreign currency are exempt from VAT (17 percent).

Visas and Passports

Tourists are required to hold passports valid for Israel, which are valid for at least six months from the date of arrival. Stateless persons require a valid travel document with a return visa to the country of issue. Citizens of the US, Canada, the EU, Australia, and New Zealand do not need a visa to enter Israel, only a valid passport. For citizens of these countries, there are no special health requirements.

Those entering Israel on vacation can only stay for three months and are not allowed to work for money. Anyone wishing to enter the country for work, study, or permanent settlement must apply for the appropriate visa at an Israeli Diplomatic or Consular Mission before leaving their own country.

All visitors to Israel, including diplomats, are required to fill out an entry form, AL-17, upon arrival. This form should be supplied on the flight to Israel. Visitors who plan on continuing to Muslim countries (except Egypt and Jordan) after their visit to Israel should ask the frontier control officer to put the entry stamp on this form instead of in their passports, as you may subsequently be refused entry into countries hostile toward Israel if an Israeli stamp appears on the passport.

Tourists wishing to stay in Israel longer than three months must obtain an extension of stay, which may be obtained through any Ministry of Interior district office with an appointment ahead of time.

Weights & Measures

Everything in Israel is metric, from kilometers to liters and grams.

Women travelers

It is generally safe for women traveling alone. Local men may pester women, but won't usually touch and will get the message if clearly given the cold shoulder. Women should dress modestly in religious areas and Jerusalem's Old City.

חוות זית המדבר
مزرعة زايت همدبار
Desert Olive Farm

חוות נחל בוקר
مزرعة ناحال بوكير
Boker Valley Vineyards

Street signs in Israel are often presented in three languages: Hebrew, Arabic and English

LANGUAGE

Hebrew is the ancient Semitic language of the Old Testament, closely related to Arabic. Used only for prayer by Orthodox Jews over the centuries and referred to as the 'Holy tongue', Hebrew was adapted to modern life at the end of the 19th century by secular Jews as part of the political Zionist movement. Uniquely, the language has been successfully revived and has taken root as the national language of Israel.

Hebrew script is descended from Phoenician, which also gave rise to the Greek, Roman and Cyrillic alphabets. The Hebrew letters derive from their original pictorial meanings: alef and bet (which gave us the word "alphabet," via Greek) are, respectively, a bull's head and a house.

Almost all signs in Israel have English as well as Hebrew and often Arabic letters but there is no standard transliteration from Hebrew to English. Thus one has: 'Acre,' 'Akko', and 'Acco'; 'Elat', 'Elath' and 'Eilat'; 'Ashqelon' and 'Ashkelon'; 'S'fat', 'Zefat', 'Tzfat', and 'Safed' etc.

Useful words and phrases

Almost without exception Israelis speak some English, but just in case:

Essential expressions
Yes *ken*
No *lo*
Okay *beseder*

Please *bevakasha*
Thank you *toda*
good *tov*
bad *ra*
and/or *ve/o*

Greetings
(all-purpose hello and goodbye) *shalom*
Good morning *boker tov*
Good evening *erev tov*
Goodnight *lyla tov*
Goodbye *lehitra-ot*
Sorry! *slikha*
How are you? *ma shlomcha* [m] *ma shlomach* [f]
Don't mention it *eyn be-ad ma*
Happy birthday *yom huledet same-akh*
Congratulations! *mazal tov*
Good luck *b'hatzlacha*

Communication difficulties
Do you speak English? [m] *ata medaber anglit* [f] *at medaberet anglit*
I don't speak much Hebrew [m] *ani lo medaber harbe ivrit* [f] *ani lo medaberet harbe ivrit*
Could you speak more slowly? [m]: *tukhal ledaber yoter le-at* [f] *tukhli ledaber yoter le-at*
Please write it down [m] *bevakasha ktov et ze* [f] *bevakasha kitvi et ze*
Can you translate this for me? [m] *tukhal letargem et ze bishvli* [f] *tukhli letargem et ze bishvli*

Old Jaffa

What does this mean? *ma zot omeret*
I understand [m] *ani mevin* [f] *mevina*
I don't understand [m] *ani lo mevin* [f] *mevina*
Do you understand? [m] *ata mevin* [f] *at mevina*

Emergencies
Help! *hatzilu*
Go away! *lekh mipo*
Leave me alone! *azov oti*
Stop thief! *ganav*
Call the police! *haz-ek-mishtara*
Get a doctor! *kra lerofe*
Fire! *srefa*
I'm ill *ani khole*
I'm lost *ta-iti baderekh*
Can you help me? *tukhal la-azor li*

Exclamations
At last! *sof sof*
Go on [m] *tamshikh* [f] *tamshikhi*
Nonsense! *shtuyot*
That's true *ze nakhon*
No way! *beshum ofen lo*
How are things? *eykh ha-inyanim*
Fine *tov*
Great *sababa*
Not bad *lo ra*
Not good *lo tov*
Terrible *nora*
You look great! *ata nir-e nifla*
Why's that? *madu-a ze*
Why not? *madu-a lo*

Everyday words
mobile phone *nayad*
to phone *le-talfen*

credit card *kartis ashrai*
cash *mezumun*
ATM *caspomat*
post office *doar*
stamps *bulim*
envelopes *ma-atafot*
writing paper *neyar ktiva*
map *mapa*
book *sefer*
newspaper *iton*
magazine *magazin*
chocolate bar *tavlat shokolad*
pen *et*
how much? *kama?*

Sights
Old City *ha-ir ha-atika*
ruins *ha-khoravot*
museum *ha-muze-on*
art gallery *galeriyat ha-omanut*
theatre *ha-te-atron*
historic site *ha-atar ha-histori*
park *ha-park*

Eating out
Can you recommend a good restaurant? *tukhal lehamlitz al mis-ada tova*
inexpensive *zola*
café *beyt kafe*
restaurant *mis-ada*
Middle Eastern *mizrakhit*
Italian *italkit*
Chinese *sinit*
vegetarian *tzimkhonit*
vegan *tivoni*
pizzeria *pitzeriya*
steakhouse *mis-adat stekim*
soup *marak*

Sign encouraging women to dress modestly in Me'a She'arim

St Peter's fish *amnun*
cod *bakala*
trout *forel*
salmon *salamon*
shrimp/prawns *khasilonim*
omelet *khavita*
eggs *beytzim*
beef *bakar*
chicken *of*
duck *barvaz*
lamb *tale*
carrots *gezer*
cabbage *kruv*
green beans *she-u-it yeruka*
peas *afuna*
mushrooms *pitriyot*
rice/pasta *orez/itriyot*
potatoes/fries *tapudim/chips*
fruit juice *mitz perot*
milk *khalav*
bread *lekhem*
butter *khem-a*
rolls *lakhmaniyot*
toast *tost*
honey *dvash*
jam *riba*
marmalade *ribat tapuzim*
lemon *limom*
mustard *khardal*
salt/pepper *melakh/pilpel*
sugar *sukar*
ketchup *ketchup*
mayonnaise *mayonez*
knife/fork *sakin/mazleg*
spoon *kaf*
plate *tzalakhat*
cup/glass *sefel/kos*
napkin *mapit*

Where are the restrooms? *eyfo hash-erutim*
The check, please *kheshbon bevakasha*

Drinks
beer *bira*
wine *yayin*
red/white *adom/lavan*
dry/sweet *yavesh/matok*
mineral water *mayim mineraliyim*

Travel
airport *nemal hate-ufa*
taxi *monit*
train *rakevet*
bus *otobus*
station/bus stop *takhanat*
one-way ticket *bekivun ekhad*
round trip *halokh vashov*
where is? *eyfo?*
right *yemin*
left *smol*
straight *yashar*

Colors
white *lavan*
black *shakhor*
red *adom*
pink *varod*
blue *kakhol*
purple *sagol*
yellow *tzahov*
green *yarok*
orange *katom*

Numbers
zero *efes*
one *ekhad*

Beware of camels near the road

two *shnayim*
three *shlosha*
four *arba-a*
five *khamisha*
six *shisha*
seven *shiv-a*
eight *shmona*
nine *tish-a*
ten *asara*
twenty *esrim*
hundred *me-a*
thousand *elef*
million *milyon*

Days
Sunday *yom rishon*
Monday *yom sheni*
Tuesday *yom shlishi*
Wednesday *yom revi-i*
Thursday *yom khamishi*
Friday *yom shishi*
Saturday *shabat*

Dates
yesterday *etmol*
today *hayom*
tomorrow *makhar*
next week *hashavu-a haba*

month *codesh*

Accommodations
I have a reservation *yesh li hazmana*
May I see the room? *efshar lir-ot et hakheder*
The air conditioning doesn't work *ha mizug avir lo po-el*
There is no hot water/toilet paper *eyn mayim khamim/neyar to-alet*
My room has not been made up *lo sidru et hakheder sheli*
I've locked myself out of my room *sagarti et atzmi mikhutz lakheder*
I'd like to move to another room *ani rotze la-avor lekheder akher*
I'd like to speak to the manager *ani rotze ledaber im hamenahel*
Are there any messages for me? *yesh hoda-ot bishvili*

Payments
May I have my check, please? *efshar lekabel et hakheshbon bevakasha*
I think there's a mistake in this check *ani kkoshev sheyesh ta-ut bakheshbon*
Could I have a receipt, please? *efshar latet li kabala bevakasha*

A still from the 1973 film Jesus Christ Superstar

BOOKS AND FILM

There is a huge amount of literature and cinema set in Israel, beginning of course with the Bible itself. In modern times, dozens of books and movies are based on the stories of biblical characters and events, some of the films actually set in Israel, such as *Jesus Christ Superstar*, while for the most part shot elsewhere, like the 2018 *Samson*, which was made in South Africa.

From the late 19th century, writers such as Mark Twain and Gustav Flaubert wrote about their travels to the Holy Land. From the 20th century onward, there have been a large number of books and movies relating to the emergence of political Zionism, the establishment of Israel, the resurrection of the Hebrew language, unique Israeli institutions like the kibbutz, and of course the Israeli-Palestinian conflict, ranging from thrillers and war movies to spy and espionage films.

There is also a rich store of Israeli literature and cinema. Israeli writer Shumel Agnon was awarded the Nobel Prize in Literature in 1966. Among the current crop of eminent Israeli writers are Amos Oz, A.B. Yehoshua, and David Grossman. The late Batya Gur was Israel's finest detective novelist. Emerging young writers include Etgar Keret and Nevo Eshkol. Modern Israeli cinema and TV includes a range of award-winning movies and TV series.

Books

Altneuland (Old New Land) by Theodor Herzl. Written in the late 19th century, Herzl's vision of a return to Zion inspired the establishment of Israel half a century later.

The Bible (Old Testament and New Testament) – in a diverse number of editions.

The Bridal Canopy by Shmuel Agnon. Written in 1931, this is considered the first-ever classic in the modern Hebrew language by the Nobel Prize winner.

The Case for Israel by Alan Dershowitz. As Israel comes under increasing fire from the BDS movement for its very existence, the legendary left-wing US defence lawyer states the case for Zionism.

Diary of Anne Frank. Set in Nazi-occupied Amsterdam, this tragic story will help visitors understand what makes Israelis tick.

Durable Peace by Benjamin Netanyahu. The Israeli Prime Minister's right-wing vision of coexistence with the Palestinians.

Judas by Amos Oz. One of the more recent novels by the Israeli writer explores the character of the biblical traitor through a tortured story about a student, his love, and an old man, set in 1950s Jerusalem.

The Liberated Bride by A.B. Yehoshua. One of the best-loved novels of the eminent Israeli writer.

The Little Drummer Girl by John Le Carre. The esteemed British spy novelist's take on the Israel-Palestinian con-

An advertising poster for Foxtrot

flict, set against the backdrop of the 1982 Israel-Lebanon War.

Murder on a Kibbutz A Communal Case by Batya Gur. One of a series of entertaining detective novels that also offers a fascinating insight into the country's communal complexities.

The New Middle East by Shimon Peres. The late Israeli Prime Minister's left-wing vision of a peaceful Middle East.

To the End of the Land by David Grossman. A fictional story of emotional anguish, based on the death of Grossman's son in the Second Lebanon War in 2006.

Start Up Nation by Dan Senor and Saul Singer. The story of Israel's economic miracle traces the success of Israel's famous high-tech industries.

Suddenly a Knock at the Door by Etgar Keret. One of the most recent enchanting collections of short stories by this internationally popular Israeli writer.

World Cup Wishes by Eshkol Nevo. Absorbing novel about young Israelis set against the backdrop of the 1998 World Cup finals in France.

Movies and TV series

The Angel (2018) An American-Israeli spy thriller about the role played by Egyptian President Nasser's son-in-law in the lead up to the Yom Kippur War in 1973.

Beaufort (2007) An Israeli movie, based on a novel by Ron Leshem, about the final days of Israel's occupation of Lebanon, set in the stunningly picturesque Crusader fortress of Beaufort.

Cast a Giant Shadow (1966) Kirk Douglas wins independence for Israel in Melville Shavelson's movie about Colonel Mickey Marcus, the US officer who fought for Israel before being killed by friendly fire because he couldn't speak Hebrew.

Entebbe (2018) Jose Padilha's movie is the latest of many attempts to depict the legendary successful rescue of Israeli hostages in Uganda by the Israeli Defence Forces in the 1976 raid.

Exodus (1960) Paul Newman wins independence for Israel in Otto Preminger's version of Leon Uris's epic novel.

Fauda (2015–18) Immensely popular Israeli TV spy-thriller series about the Israel-Palestinian conflict, which has enjoyed international popularity after being picked up by Netflix.

Foxtrot (2017) Directed by Samuel Maoz, the movie tells the anguished story of a middle class Tel Aviv couple whose son is killed in action in the Israeli army.

Jesus Christ Superstar (1973) Set among the stunning landscapes of the Judean Desert and Dead Sea, this is Norman Jewison's cinematic version of the popular Time Rice and Andrew Lloyd Webber musical.

The Little Drummer Girl (1984 and 2018) Roy Hill's 1984 version of John Le Carre's novel has Diane Keaton recruited as a Mossad agent. Re-made by the BBC in 2018 as a mini-series.

A Tale of Love and Darkness (2015) Natalie Portman directs and stars in Amos Oz's tortured autobiographical novel about the suicide of his mother.

ABOUT THIS BOOK

This *Explore Guide* has been produced by the editors of Insight Guides, whose books have set the standard for visual travel guides since 1970. With top-quality photography and authoritative recommendations, these guidebooks bring you the very best routes and itineraries in the world's most exciting destinations.

BEST ROUTES

The routes in the book provide something to suit all budgets, tastes and trip lengths. As well as covering the destination's many classic attractions, the itineraries track lesser-known sights, and there are also excursions for those who want to extend their visit outside the city. The routes embrace a range of interests, so whether you are an art fan, a gourmet, a history buff or have kids to entertain, you will find an option to suit.

We recommend reading the whole of a route before setting out. This should help you to familiarise yourself with it and enable you to plan where to stop for refreshments – options are shown in the 'Food and Drink' box at the end of each tour.

For our pick of the tours by theme, consult Recommended Routes for… (see pages 6–7).

INTRODUCTION

The routes are set in context by this introductory section, giving an overview of the destination to set the scene, plus background information on food and drink, shopping and more, while a succinct history timeline highlights the key events over the centuries.

DIRECTORY

Also supporting the routes is a Directory chapter, with a clearly organised A–Z of practical information, our pick of where to stay while you are there and select restaurant listings; these eateries complement the more low-key cafés and restaurants that feature within the routes and are intended to offer a wider choice for evening dining. Also included here are some nightlife listings, plus a handy language guide and our recommendations for books and films about the destination.

ABOUT THE AUTHOR

Simon Griver is a Jerusalem-based journalist who specializes in writing about Israel. He is Managing Editor of *Globes*, an Israeli financial news website. Simon also regularly writes about Israel for newspapers and websites worldwide, and has written several other Insight Guides, including *Insight Guide Israel* and *Insight Pocket Guide Israel*. Born and educated in England, Simon has lived in Israel since 1978.

CONTACT THE EDITORS

We hope you find this Explore Guide useful, interesting and a pleasure to read. If you have any questions or feedback on the text, pictures or maps, please do let us know. If you have noticed any errors or outdated facts, or have suggestions for places to include on the routes, we would be delighted to hear from you. Please drop us an email at hello@insightguides.com. Thanks!

CREDITS

Explore Jerusalem and Tel Aviv
Editor: Tom Fleming
Author: Simon Griver
Head of DTP and Pre-Press: Rebeka Davies
Managing Editor: Carine Tracanelli
Picture Editor: Tom Smyth
Cartography: Carte
Photo credits: Alamy 7MR, 24/25, 42, 47, 78, 78/79, 102, 109, 110, 128, 129; Atef Safadi/EPA/REX/Shutterstock 24; AWL Images 4/5T, 8/9T, 28/29T, 94/95T; Dana Friedlander/Israeli Ministry of Tourism 4MC, 19, 64/65T; Getty Images 12, 25L, 26, 27, 38/39, 54/55, 80, 81, 82/83; Haim Yosef 6MC; iStock 6TL, 6ML, 10, 11T, 14/15, 23, 28MC, 33, 52B, 84B; Itamar Grinberg 8ML, 8MR, 28ML; Itamar Grinberg/Israeli Ministry of Tourism. 84/85, 87, 88, 90, 91T, 90/91T, 93L, 92/93, 113, 120; Jim Hollander/EPA/REX/Shutterstock 111; Leonardo 28ML, 94ML, 94MC, 94MR, 94MR, 94MC, 94ML, 96, 97, 98, 99, 100, 101, 103, 105; Mordagan/Israel Ministry of Tourism 89; Noam Chen/Israel Ministry of Tourism 8MC, 28MR, 34, 35L, 36, 40T, 48, 112, 118; Nowitz Photography/Apa Publications 4ML, 4MC, 7T, 7M, 7MR, 8MR, 20/21, 28MC, 32, 34/35, 40B, 50/51, 58, 61L, 84T, 85L, 86, 91MC, 92, 115, 121, 123, 124, 125, 126, 127; Shutterstock 1, 4ML, 4MR, 4MR, 6BC, 8ML, 8MC, 11B, 13L, 12/13, 16, 17L, 16/17, 18, 20, 21L, 22, 28MR, 30/31, 37, 41, 43, 44, 45L, 44/45, 46, 49, 50, 51L, 52T, 53, 56, 57, 59, 60, 60/61, 62/63, 64, 65MC, 65T, 66, 67, 68, 69MC, 69T, 68/69T, 70B, 70T, 71, 72, 73, 74, 75L, 74/75, 76, 77, 79L, 104, 106, 107, 108, 114, 116, 117, 119, 122
Cover credits: iStock (main and bottom) Shutterstock (back)

DISTRIBUTION

UK, Ireland and Europe
Apa Publications (UK) Ltd
sales@insightguides.com
United States and Canada
Ingram Publisher Services
ips@ingramcontent.com
Australia and New Zealand
Woodslane
info@woodslane.com.au
Southeast Asia
Apa Publications (Singapore) Pte
singaporeoffice@insightguides.com
Worldwide
Apa Publications (UK) Ltd
sales@insightguides.com

SPECIAL SALES, CONTENT LICENSING AND COPUBLISHING

Insight Guides can be purchased in bulk quantities at discounted prices. We can create special editions, personalised jackets and corporate imprints tailored to your needs.
sales@insightguides.com
www.insightguides.biz

INDEX